P9-EMC-066

Accounting Theory

One of the outstanding accounting theoreticians of the twentieth century, Carl Thomas Devine exhibited a breadth and depth of knowledge few in the field of accounting have equalled. This book collects together eight previously unpublished essays on accounting theory written by Professor Devine.

Professor Devine passed away in 1998, prior to the significant scandals that have plagued accounting and business since the collapse of Enron and Arthur Andersen. Many of the essays collected here are particularly important given these events. The first three essays are devoted to ethics and provide profound insights into the importance of a profession's ethical presuppositions. The book then presents essays which provide a critical examination of the relevance of hermeneutics and deconstruction to an understanding of accounting practice and an analysis of the academic "game" particularly with respect to Professor Devine's experiences in the Florida university system. The final essay in the volume is devoted to a critique of rational choice theory applications in accounting.

Revisiting and building upon themes developed in earlier work, this collection of essays will be essential reading for accounting historians, accounting theoreticians, and all those interested in the work of Carl Thomas Devine.

The late Harvey S. Hendrickson received his Ph.D. from the University of Minnesota in 1963. He served on the faculties at SUNY – Buffalo, and The Florida State University before he began his long and distinguished service of 29 years at Florida International University. Professor Hendrickson published scholarly articles in leading accounting journals such as *The Accounting Review* and *Journal of Accounting and Public Policy*. He also published articles in leading practitioner journals. He edited the previous collection of Professor Devine's essays, *Carl Thomas Devine: Essays in Accounting Theory – A Capstone*.

Paul F. Williams is Professor of Accounting at North Carolina State University. He has published articles in a number of scholarly journals and is the Associate Editor of *Accounting and the Public Interest*, the Public Interest Section of the American Accounting Association's on-line journal. He is a founding member of the Association for Integrity in Accounting.

Routledge new works in accounting history
Series editors:
Richard Brief, Leonard N. Stern
School of Business, New York University

Garry Carnegie
Deakin University, Australia

John Richard Edwards
Cardiff Business School, UK

Richard Macve
London School of Economics, UK

Accounting Theory

Essays by Carl Thomas Devine

HF
6625
D 458
2004
web

Edited by
Harvey S. Hendrickson and
Paul F. Williams

Routledge
Taylor & Francis Group

LONDON AND NEW YORK

First published 2004
by Routledge
11 New Fetter Lane, London EC4P 4EE

Simultaneously published in the USA and Canada
by Routledge
29 West 35th Street, New York, NY 10001

Routledge is an imprint of the Taylor & Francis Group

© 2004 The Estate of Carl Thomas Devine for individual essays; the
Estate of Harvey S. Hendrickson, and Paul F. Williams for editorial
matter and selection

Typeset in Sabon by
Newgen Imaging Systems (P) Ltd, Chennai, India
Printed and bound in Great Britain by
TJ International Ltd, Padstow, Cornwall

All rights reserved. No part of this book may be reprinted or
reproduced or utilised in any form or by any electronic,
mechanical, or other means, now known or hereafter
invented, including photocopying and recording, or in any
information storage or retrieval system, without permission in
writing from the publishers.

British Library Cataloguing in Publication Data
A catalogue record for this book is available
from the British Library

Library of Congress Cataloging in Publication Data
Devine, Carl Thomas.
    Accounting theory: essays by Carl Thomas Devine / edited by
Harvey S. Hendrickson and Paul F. Williams.
        p. cm.
    Includes bibliographical references and index.
    1. Accounting. I. Hendrickson, Harvey S. II. Williams, Paul F.,
1947– III. Title.

HF5625.D458 2004
657'.01–dc22   2003026222

ISBN 0–415–30988–3

Contents

Carl Thomas Devine (1911–98)

In loving memory of Harvey S. Hendrickson (1928–2001)

Harvey's work on these essays, up to his death, seem to punctuate an excerpt from his high school valedictorian speech, "Life means growth and growth means life. We must advance or we stagnate." But his intellectual pursuits were only surpassed by his love for his family. He will reside forever in their hearts and minds.

His family,
Rosanne, Mary, Erik, and Elise

Editor's preface

This volume of eight essays provides a culmination of a sort to the careers of two exceptional accounting scholars: Carl T. Devine and Harvey S. Hendrickson. The editing of this seventh volume of Carl Devine's essays was the project Harvey was diligently laboring at when he passed away. It has been a singular honor for me to add some finishing touches to Harvey's work in order to get this final collection of Carl's essays into print.

Both Carl and Harvey were of an era in accounting scholarship when ideas were the coin of the realm rather than methodological dogmas. Carl and Harvey were both lovers of ideas and of learning; they infused the seemingly mundane field of accounting with the intellectual vitality they gathered from their far-ranging interests in virtually every discipline in the academy. Dierdre McCloskey, the noted economic historian, gives an account of the life of one of her scholarly exemplars, the distinguished economic historian, Alexander Gerschenkron. In her book *If You're So Smart*, she devotes chapter five to telling "The Scholar's Story," which is the story of her intellectual hero. One particular passage is my favorite because every time I read it, I am reminded of the two men whose work is represented by this volume:

> Waiting in Gerschenkron's office for an interview one day a graduate student received from the nearest of numerous stacks of books and magazines a lesson in the scholarly life, the sort of lesson that professors forget they give. The stack contained a book of plays in Greek, a book on non-Euclidean geometry, a book of chess problems, numerous statistical tomes, journals of literature and science, several historical works in various languages, and, at the bottom of it all, two feet deep, a well-worn copy of *Mad* magazine. Here was a scholar.[1]

Indeed, Carl and Harvey were scholars worthy of the name.

This collection of essays was written mostly in 1996 and 1997, just before Carl became too ill to carry on. Chapters 6 and 7 were written earlier: Chapter 7 in 1991 and Chapter 6 was likely written much earlier than that. This volume is even more a potpourri than the six previous volumes. Carl revisits some themes he pursued in earlier essays; many of the essays in this volume act as addenda to previous ones. A reading of Carl's earlier volumes would be in order so that one can place these essays in their appropriate contexts. These essays once again demonstrate Carl's breadth and depth of understanding and his intellectual integrity, which Harvey obviously admired so much. That a person in his mid-80s wrote these essays is a testament to the intellectual power Carl possessed.

The ordering of the essays is as Harvey decided they should be arranged. The first three generally deal with the subject of ethics – a major focus of Carl's thinking throughout his career. These essays are particularly topical at the moment and would be worthwhile reading for any serious student of accounting, practitioner, and academic alike, since they provide profound insights into the importance of a profession's ethical presuppositions. The next two continue Carl's critical examination of hermeneutics and deconstruction, which are his principal preoccupations in volume six.

Chapters 6 and 7 are very much editorials. Chapter 6 is a brief essay on academic publishing and Chapter 7 is a lengthy discussion on higher education, which reflects Carl's very personal experiences with higher education in the state of Florida. Chapter 8 is incomplete; Carl was not particularly pleased with the progress he was making in elaborating his thoughts more on rational choice theory and subjective probability. He never finished it, but Harvey decided what of it that was completed should be published.

Harvey and I have tried to locate the sources for all references Carl made; we have been mostly successful, but there are some references we are not certain about. Where these exist, we have provided editor's notes providing our best guesses as to the proper source. The editing we have done has been fastidious at preserving Carl's original language. Were one to subject this text to a Microsoft audit of spelling and grammar it would look like a Christmas wreath. Carl uses many words that are words only within the particular disciplines that coined them or they are coinages of Carl's own creation. Lengthy passages that might be "improved" with editing were left as Carl's notations on the originals indicate he intended them to be left. The text has also not been edited for political correctness, for example, Carl uses the masculine pronouns throughout. Obvious misspellings and typographical errors have been corrected, but Harvey and I have conscientiously retained the text as Carl wrote it. How that text is interpreted will obviously be left up to the readers.

Note

1 McCloskey, D. N., *If You're So Smart: The Narrative of Economic Expertise*, Chicago: The University of Chicago Press, 1990, p. 75.

1 Responsibilities, ethics, and legitimacy

This essay is concerned with the development of professional ethics in service institutions. The discussion deals with the transition from simple acceptance of definite responsibilities in functional relationships to the primal teleological problem of selecting among competing groups with their own semi-independent value systems and conflicting ends in view (objectives). In the process, a profession must establish the legitimacy of its own ethical system along with sufficient authority to command conformance.

It is assumed here that the needs of those using the service are potentially conflicting and cannot be satisfied in full so that valuations and rankings are required. The code of professional ethics then becomes an explicit statement of the value system of a profession with sufficient authority to demand compliance. It is at this point that a service organization moves beyond simple acceptance of responsibilities from a consistent outside source and develops the inner dynamics (forces) necessary to establish a profession.[1]

The further contention of this chapter is that the chief functions of ethical codes are indirectly related to the need to fill in the areas not covered by legal and other authoritative pronouncements. This view has dominated traditional discourse and perhaps has overemphasized the need for some device to cover the inevitable loose ends. Certainly, the application of broader and more general codes cannot cover all possible instances and must leave some discretion to lower decision centers. Often these lower-level guidelines are little more than functional statements with simple acceptance of responsibilities and rules for carrying out specific duties. With an accepted authoritative hierarchy, the term ethics is too inclusive and it is recommended that the term be reserved for teleological problems that arise from the need to preserve equity among differing individuals. *Codes* of ethics then become formalized lists of appropriate behaviors to achieve coordinated objectives.

This adjustment of specific value systems to one another and to higher directives is a necessary condition for social living and is related to legislative edicts and to the exercise of authority generally. Thus any functioning society must meld all sorts of conflicting value systems and objectives into a more or less consistent pattern. Members of a democratic society, for example, must be willing to compromise and adjust some of their immediate aims and values, but they must retain sufficient shared values that are compromised with reluctance in order to remain governable and avoid failure from sheer diversity. While this compromising process of continual grinding and adjusting is of later interest, the greater interest here is with the teleologic problem of selecting among competing interests and establishing the legitimacy of the professional value system.

With this framework, ethical problems do not arise unless there are choices that involve different individuals. The necessary bargaining process usually means that professional ethics are the result of compromise with all sorts of benefits and sacrifices for the parties involved, and once the code is accepted the sacrifices fall on parties who are forced to modify their personal objectives to conform. Traditional cost–benefit analysis is of little use in these cases because sacrifices often are imposed on certain groups while benefits run to others. (The reader no doubt is aware that ethical decisions often are biased – especially when outcomes favor the person making the decision.) Clearly some controls or alternative processes for formulating professional codes is essential.

Ethics and simple responsibilities

The relationship of duties and responsibilities to ethical systems always has been ambiguous. In the simplest sense, an ethical code can be viewed as a list of responsibilities that are involved in any problematic situation. For example, with effective socialization and definite status levels the appropriate principles of action for role members may be inferred from the customs and usage of the culture.[2] It seems therefore that so long as the service nature of the profession is understood – the professional mission known – the appropriate code of ethics is little more than an ordinary tabulation of these constructed responsibilities and their corresponding duties. In this view, ethics reduces to little more than establishing behaviors to accomplish the mission.

There is an important relationship between responsibilities and codes of ethics, but to identify them is to be overly simplistic. In the least complicated case this approach reduces to the task of finding a recognized superior (host) and then deciding without ambiguity to accept and follow the superior's system of values. The task then reduces to tracing probable consequences of decisions and actions in terms of their ability to satisfy the conditions set by the master. Yet even with an acknowledged and unambiguous superior, problems arise in weighing and evaluating unless all consequences can be satisfied. (Consider the endless controversies among Church Fathers over the relative importance of various transgressions.) Furthermore even with a single commander all possible choices and trade-offs can never be specified. Only with a homogeneous profession with identical values and known probability assessments about consequences can the problem be removed even in the simplest cases.

It is widely understood in all hierarchical societies that guidelines limit subordinates at all levels and that much of the work of subordinates is in the form of responsibility for following accepted guidelines. We already have commented on the serious problems of identifying dominant groups and giving appropriate attention to minority demands. A further difficult question arises with any residual freedom that remains at subordinate (professional) levels. If by definition these actions are *not* covered by accepted rules from above, what indeed does govern the nature of the responsibilities taken? Consistency? Consistency with what? In what respects? Precisely what is the meaning of consistency in this situation? Who is to decide? Even simple responsibility–duty relationships in uncomplicated hierarchies are far from simple.

While the problems of responsibility and duty are difficult enough and often require serious trade-offs and complicated interpretations, the more difficult problems arise with the selection of multiple hosts and beneficiaries. These decisions go beyond simple agency and bring the resolution of interpersonal conflict directly to the front. Teleology with some *independent* "discernment of the good" replaces simple unilateral trade-offs.[3] Indeed, the problem is not restricted to service organizations because all individuals must make choices among numerous and often pressing responsibilities. In the ordinary course of living an individual must make choices among responsibilities to his/her spouse, children, church, fraternity/sorority, and to humanity itself. Political responsibilities come from townships, counties, states, and from federal citizenship. Clearly, simple responsibilities soon become ethical problems of the first magnitude. Once again the tired old question: What does it mean to be a human being?

Finally the obligation to use abrasive forms of persuasion – even in major political protests – needs exploration. From the usual perspective, the obligation to protest arises from dissatisfaction with value impositions from some superior force and from a powerful need to modify these values for greater consistency with alternative value systems. A prime example is afforded by war trials where broad humanitarian values are in conflict with the values of a political state. The right-to-revolution arguments usually assume that the possible atrocities of revolution are preferred over submission to the values of the dominating group.

Interpersonal – multiple hosts

The intention here is to support and reinforce my belief that the term "ethics" should be restricted to potential and actual interpersonal conflicts.[4] Essential to the argument is that so long as a service institution has only one outside host, no ethical judgment is needed except in the rudimentary sense of weighing responsibilities and regulating internal relationships. In short, the contention is that professional ethics develop with multiusers so that choices must be made in an interpersonal arena. It is this task of judging and compromising that demands ethical judgment and develops the heralded "dynamics" of service institutions. Thus, a profession needs to develop its own system of values to evaluate and influence the objectives of these diverse users. Clearly, the individual value systems of each legitimate and contending party cannot provide an acceptable standard so that some relatively independent set of value standards is needed to guide the necessary choices. As with all guidelines the ethical codes of all service professions must yield sacrifices (costs) to some users and benefits to others. Clearly, the calculation of these costs and benefits require some relatively independent standard.

The need for ethical codes to preserve equity among differing but deserving groups usually is taken for granted and often is set forth as *the* generalized objective for all service professions. Nagging questions remain. How do the leaders recognize equity and go about attaining it? Is the term "equity" like the concept of justice too idealized and vague to serve as a practical standard? Can any part of cost–benefit analysis be utilized? It is of course possible to adopt the self-interest ethics of one of the contending parties, but the accepted practice has been to construct a new composite value perspective from the needs of all and to use this perspective to assess individual sacrifices and benefits. This new perspective and its rules for application become the new code of ethics for the semi-independent profession.

The distinction between a list of responsibilities and a code of ethical behavior is similar to the usual distinction between functional and teleological inquiry. It has been emphasized that in the former case, the value system of the host is accepted and the consequences of various behaviors are examined to determine whether they further accepted objectives. Clearly, even in the simple functional case, responsibilities and therefore professional responses may be conflicting and some choices must be made about appropriate duties to discharge acknowledged responsibilities. Furthermore, expected consequences for each alternative may not be clear so that even uni-host decisions may become complicated. In the second case (teleological choice), the situation is more complex and some assessment of the *common* welfare is needed. This discernment of the common good is essential for creating a master value system and for assembling the specifics that make up codes of ethics.

In this context, Arrington and Puxty are correct in criticizing my previous approach that overemphasized guidelines for satisfying an accepted master rather than the more difficult task of selecting (constructing) a composite leader. The important area for the application of values and ethical discernment is clearly in the process of constructing a host from deserving claimants by weighing, ordering, and melding their worthy objectives.[5]

Some major accounting writers (e.g. Churchman and Mattessich) have insisted that the objectives of a profession are exogenous and determined largely if not entirely by the objectives of outside groups. It certainly is true that any service profession or activity exists to serve the needs of others and is not isolated from its environment. But too often, advocates of this position insist that the accounting profession respond primarily by accepting responsibilities from a single authoritative source. With these conditions, ethics for the profession becomes little more than a listing of duties and regulations for internal relations. Certainly little or no room is left for developing the coercive and authoritative inner dynamics that usually are associated with professional integrity. In practice, the selection of a leader requires value judgments and the construction of a composite. In the process, some potential leadership groups are favored and others disadvantaged with the objectives of all legitimate groups often compromised and blended. In D. R. Scott's terms, the accounting profession has a force of its own and is "fraught" with problems of fairness, justice, and truth for all contending parties.[6]

In the absence of completely homogeneous influences, some power must reside in the profession. It is no longer correct to think of a profession as a senseless errand boy working for a single special interest group. It is tempting to argue that the older and more established the profession, the stronger its independence and its inner dynamic power. This relationship so far as I know has not been researched, and the hypothesis that professional power varies inversely with the homogeneity of shared values may be more interesting.

It is now fashionable to argue that the contents of professional codes of ethics must be consistent in some sense with the objectives of those with broader or stronger authority. Precisely what does consistency mean in this context? Presumably, it means that the consequences of following professional guidelines must further the objectives of some constructed (composite) authority in some way. It is likely that influential groups make compromises through the usual horse-trading process, and turn over the coordination and enforcement of compromise guidelines to the profession. The profession in turn delegates some freedom to lower groups. Each subordinate group then enjoys some limited areas of freedom and thus is able to exercise some power. The individual and his/her conscience represent a code of ethics at its lowest level.

Individuals are members of all sorts of influencing groups whose objectives and ethical values must be melded into their own systems of personal values. The goals of these organizations may be in conflict and the individuals themselves may integrate them poorly. The result may well be an extension of the old-fashioned concept of anomie with persistent but ambivalent goals and insufficient institutional means to satisfy them. In any case, an individual's own conscience usually is composed of bizarre mixtures of values from church dogmas, family customs, secret-society rituals, school indoctrination, media hype, and pressures from state and country. Certainly, possibilities for poorly integrated personalities abound in all pluralistic social groups.

Establishing legitimacy and authority

A code of ethics must possess authority to be an effective device for social control, and it must establish credibility to gain effective authority. Credibility in turn depends on persuasion to convince members that the professional code expresses their own interests. Inasmuch as some interests have been compromised and sacrificed, establishing legitimacy becomes a semi-logical process by which the consequences of following ethical guidelines is shown to be consistent with the objectives of a more important *entity* or *need*. While the usual doubts about the meaning of consistency and specification of probable consequences are important, our interest here is with the process of convincing affected parties that the suggested code of ethics should be supported despite some undesirable consequences.

The following discussion deals with justifications that appeal to semantic and methodologic devices, divine revelation, natural law (with biological and physical models), human psychology, social environment, legal and political precedents, and even to humanity itself.

Ethical justification takes numerous forms with semantic arguments being among the more popular. No one denies that words and verbal expressions help shape concepts of reality, but semantic referents often are so vague that they should influence only the most unsophisticated scholar. Unfortunately, they often end meaningful discourse and convince many otherwise sophisticated accountants. Terms such as honesty, truth, justice, fairness, equity, and clichés such as "level playing field" often are used with success even though each is ambiguous and depends entirely on perspective.

Arguments based on such symbols may have limited usefulness. They express vague ideals to which a profession might aspire, but in logical terms they tend to beg the question or encourage errors of composition and in pragmatic terms they often are nonoperational. A negative factor is that they may stop both discourse and inquiry before an understanding is reached. Thus, they often are a means for closing discourse or at the very least for limiting relevant discussion. What may seem fair and just from one perspective may seem terribly unfair and unjust from another – even atrocities such as wars may appear to be just in the minds of all combatants.

In summary, idealized semantic terms may or may not direct relevant discourse, but they clearly avoid the specific details that ethical codes are designed to control. Broad semantic arguments become useful to pragmatic professions only when they include operational instructions for adopting an appropriate perspective and some method for evaluating competing values. Unfortunately, excessive concern with specific operations sometimes can lead to a "methodolatry" in which the outcomes of applying methods become substitutes for ethical discrimination.

The most persuasive support for legitimacy may come in the form of a divine revelation that sets guidelines to which all cooperating codes of ethics must conform. Some heavenly power provides a detailed plan for the universe and conveys the specifics to human beings through various forms of revelation that include semantic devices such as the *Word* to announce and direct spiritual intervention. This master power also monitors the actions of its charges and metes out punishments and rewards so that its desires become authoritative.

Despite serious efforts to make the master ethical system explicit, some differences remain at the human level. To some the master becomes a personality who sometimes intervenes in a direct physical sense. To others the power is exerted through personal feelings, soul stirrings, and unswerving faith. Still others feel that a universal power already has settled on an Eternal Law that accounts for every action in the entire universe in a deterministic manner. The existence of this eternal plan is supported by faith and relevance, and sometimes is transmitted to humans by logical processes. The logically deducted representations are incomplete and imperfect, but together they constitute the Natural Law. With or without logical deduction, the Eternal Law is transmitted by revelations that require hermeneutical interpretation. An individual's own interpretation then provides his/her *conscience* and intuitive feeling for right and wrong with which all codes of ethics must conform.[7]

Ethicists with less mystical grounding but in need of secure foundations have created a less spiritual basis for justification. This concept of nature (and the resulting natural man) has its own inexorable laws that are no less coercive. Many consider these natural laws to be more convincing than religious edicts because the consequences of nonconformance are more clearly revealed through direct observation. Common observation, along with interpretation and understanding, do indeed suggest powerful external forces to which human ethics and behavior must conform. While these influences often are aggregated and used to support derived natural laws, they seldom are associated with spiritual leaders and supernatural foundations. Thus, many traditional scientists seem to be unaware that science itself is based on sheer faith and are content to abandon all theistic overtones. Their faith depends primarily on observation and man's ability to discover nature's laws that they are able to coordinate to support ethical codes of behavior.

There are further divergences among those who wish to ground human ethics in natural phenomena. The less successful of these groups support their values through physical and mechanical analogies. Faith in input–output symmetries, liquid flows, electrical circuitry, balancing mechanisms, geometric equivalencies, energy conversions, isomorphic representations, and even representative-truth criteria afford support. To some, these physical constructions are little more than props for understanding; but to others, they are templates to which human ethics must conform. To still others the presumed physical necessities themselves become the ethics of human relationships.

Biological justification for human ethical behavior has proven to be more interesting and perhaps more productive. Many are satisfied with Darwin's simplistic random adaptation while others expand the doctrine with assumptions about gene distribution, territorial expansion, and the like. Biological necessities sometimes surface in the form of homeostatic survival, species continuity, phylogenic anthropology, ontogenic individualism, and all sorts of assumed yens, traits, inherited characteristics, and even instincts. The homeostatic assumption in particular has been an important integrating hypothesis to justify certain aspects of human ethical standards.

Within the last generation, serious attempts have been made to blend biological and mechanical models into the interesting new world of cybernetics. Here, certain operations such as feedback and control are treated as more fundamental than traditional mechanical and biological models. These scientists still are seeking a natural integrating structure to which all codes of ethics must conform. Meanwhile, their justification rests on the primacy of natural laws.

Often the search for ethical legitimacy is grounded in some perceived or constructed *human condition*. This concept is less embracing than an entire natural world so that some means are necessary to identify precisely those aspects of the natural universe that define it. Unfortunately, the human condition contains some supernatural features so that the substitution has no genuine simplification. Thus, the concept is unavoidably vague although it usually is expanded by assuming that the welfare of human beings is dominant and by constructing a more or less ideal set of conditions for satisfying these needs. This ideal set then becomes the standard to which all subordinate codes of behavior must conform. In practice the "virtues" and "ultimate goods" of ancient philosophy usually are resurrected for support. Emphasis often is on presumed ideal conditions for individuals, but such an orientation is not necessary and many humanists advocate a conception of the common good – the general welfare. In this case individual values are subordinated to (or even determined by) group well being, and the human condition becomes an idealized group condition.

Many seek legitimacy by expanding small-group and individual codes to cover the customs and mores of the dominant culture. This method of justification may be viewed as a subdivision of the more general humanistic paradigm with the restricting assumption that the historical wisdom of past cultural activities provides an acceptable ethical base. This view is optimistic about the fate of mankind and insists that the unfolding of history is in good hands and is progressing toward the ultimate objectives of human endeavor. Historical research methods and anthropological techniques become important tools for uncovering and constructing value systems appropriate for individuals and small groups. Inasmuch as this value base is derived from existing social conditions, the view is unacceptable to many young revolutionaries and apostles of the new left.

Modern social structures are highly complex so that some method must be devised to separate the desirable and undesirable features. The use of sheer existence (historical survival) is a widely used simplification. This extension of Social Darwinism remains convincing to many first-rate accountants including most followers of Littleton. This doctrine in its crudest form assumes that what exists is good and therefore should be valued and preserved. In practice, further means must be devised for recognizing existing practices whose legitimate functions no longer exist. Moreover, some attention must be given to current human needs that are not being served. In any case, the historical simplification tends to de-emphasize the need for conscious ethical judgment and indeed for ethics itself.

While dependence on present existence and historical precedent may provide a faulty ethical foundation, alternate methods for assessing cultural structures also are troubling. The usual procedure is to select some group or process in the social system to be the standard bellwether and to insist that all subordinate codes of ethics conform. Indeed such programs of simplification and subrogation to represent broader entities and populations may be unavoidable. Some limitations are clearly necessary but such a process does not guarantee a firm ethical foundation or provide specific justification. Code makers may select nonrepresentative and partisan segments, and attempt to justify their own positions by asserting consistency with cultural standards.

In practice, the simplification–subrogation method usually follows the pattern of letting legislators and related politicians make the decisions, and then accepting the legal guidelines that emerge as appropriate ethical standards. Thus, many leading senators and several presidents have attempted to defend themselves by asserting that they have done nothing unlawful and thus by implication nothing unethical. Perry Mason, a highly regarded accountant, has insisted that accounting responsibilities, over large areas, can be satisfied by following legal prescriptions.[8] Possible difficulties for this process appear at once when the ethical domain is extended. In the Nüremberg Trials, the heinous actions of certain Nazi leaders were judged by standards, said to be derived, from the ethical norms of humanity, itself. Some controversy naturally arose about the precise identity of these bedrock (uncompromisable) human values, but it is clear that ethical standards sponsored by leaders of important national states are no longer supreme. Within the last decade or two, this view has been extended into concerted international efforts to improve human rights in states where ethical patterns are inconsistent with the dominant worldview. Inquiry into the consistency of cultural values clearly is desirable even though the values necessary to support the human condition are unavoidably vague and too often are selected by the current political powers.

Conflict over the selection of appropriate reference groups has been widespread among extreme individualists and libertarians. The anarchistic and nihilistic radicals of the Berkeley New Left questioned authority at all levels and did not feel obligated to follow any politically sanctioned laws or directives. Their own codes were based on existentialism and the teachings of modern psychiatrists and thus elevated an individual's conscience to an innate standard of right and wrong. In the tradition of Sartre, no informed human being could possibly deceive himself and the humanity in all human creatures must ultimately prevail. Possible conflicts among individuals were somehow lost or resolved in a vast a priori of human goodness. To some philosophers their critical attitudes and methods were deconstructionism at its best – to others at its worst.

Marxists too are unwilling to accept the political and sociological guidelines common to capitalistic societies and continue to search for alternative bases for ethical justification. In practice, this search becomes messy although some innate human values found in proletarian cultures usually are assumed to be dominant. In the interim, while existing institutions are being rearranged, equal faith has been placed in the judgment of revolutionary leaders and the rhetoric of Marx and Engels. Faith in the judgment of both common men and leaders is apparently unbounded once the fetters of vulgar bourgeois values have been removed. Incidentally, this source of legitimacy is remarkably similar to democratic faith in the wisdom and values of the common voter. The effective democratic man too must modify his values to include compromise and other skills for democratic living.

Capitalistic economics has supplied a strong ethical influence and accountants traditionally have looked to businessmen as their reference group and role model. The needs of business organizations to procure and enhance capital, and to direct workers toward profitable ends have been paramount. Thus, accountants have concentrated on tracing debt and ownership claims, accounting for the sources and growth of present wealth, and assessing the potentials for future wealth. Accordingly, accounting guidelines usually are directed toward the reduction of dysfunctional practices and toward increasing the ability of workers to cooperate in the interest of investors and others concerned with the economic concept of wealth.

In the highly simplified world of economics, scanning the cultural and social order for acceptable objectives and simplifications continues. With the exception of an occasional welfare theorist, economists themselves have all but swept away their ethical problems by assuming that the outcomes of free-market transactions meet (or establish) adequate ethical standards. This substitute for comprehensive ethical standards has worked moderately well in the Western World and has been adopted by many modern positivist and empirical accountants. The Rochester School, for example, adopts without serious question market outcomes as adequate support for accounting principles. Accounting codes of ethics play an unimportant role, and professional discipline and values enter the equation only as one of numerous influences affecting market allocations. In the extreme market tradition, so forcibly defended by Raymond Chambers, *all* business objectives are controlled and actualized through market operations. Meanwhile accountants, like ancient Greek Warriors, must await the fates handed down by Olympian markets and adjust their behaviors with professional resignation.

In recent years, the assumptions underlying market allocations have been extended to cover contention within organizations. The outcomes of intra-firm self-interest bargaining are taken as acceptable substitutes for organizational ethics. In effect, the market ethos is expanded and again ethical codes and *professional* discipline for agents and principals are incorporated as only one-among-many influences in an agent-contractual format. Conflicts in value systems are disregarded so long as the ethics of bargaining and the market place are not violated. The ethical supremacy of a bargaining market system replaces appeals to gods, or to natural laws, or even to the necessary requirements for a just and humane society.

Finally, consider accountants who appeal to science and mathematics to justify their ethical beliefs. Those with faith in the ability of scientific methodologies to support ultimate ethical values may be divided into a group that places its faith in observational techniques, and another that emphasizes mathematical and logical model making. This split is unfortunate because it decreases support for the productive hypothetico-deductive paradigm of constant interaction between sensual observations and the structuring processes of mathematics. These accountants have great faith in the justifying powers of their methodologies but their emphasis usually is divergent. Empiricists depend largely on the foundation afforded by the assumption of an outside (natural) world and accept observational outcomes as effective ethical guidelines. Mathematical theorists also have faith in their methodological processes. They often express their simplifications and generalizations in the traditional positivist if–then format so that their models may be adapted to all sorts of external observations and subjective value systems. Extreme members of both groups sometimes assert that their investigations are value-free. Such an objective may well be undesirable and it is certainly impossible to attain. Value judgments simply abound at every step from selecting a basis for verification to deciding the scope of valid generalization.

Appeals to science for ethical justification are partially dependent on methodologies, but at bottom they too are grounded in a posited natural world with (at the minimum) statistical regularities. Accountants with a penchant for biological and physical models are influenced by the natural world, and hope to *discover* its regularities and express them as natural laws that must be obeyed. The consequences of ethical behavior must be consistent with these laws or suffer extinction. Behavioral accountants too prefer scientific methods with their emphasis on observing and predicting psychological and sociological regularities, and forming laws of behavior for natural men and their associations. The use of complicated statistical processes must not obscure this primitive grounding.

Scientific methods to some degree are polysemantic and thus closer to the newer language-based and hermeneutic approaches to knowledge. It is certainly true that reputable scientists reach only tentative conclusions, and remain open to refutation and change. On the whole, they remain faithful to their methods and firm in their support of observations and objective evidence. It seems obvious to scientists that surviving ethical guidelines for human conduct must be consistent with certain natural necessities. Rational students will agree that some guidelines lead to disaster, but many insist that there are many areas of choice with freedom to exercise subjective judgment. The important area for subjective ethical judgment concerns interpersonal conduct – not man's direct relationships to natural forces.

Mathematical and logical manipulations give a feeling of deterministic security. This feeling belies the subjective judgments that are necessary at every step from forming the model, through estimating the goodness of fit, to generalizing the outcomes. Even with the addition of probability techniques and the tentative adoption of the newer fuzzy logic, the deterministic flavor of logico-mathematics runs counter to the polysemantic interpretations of the common-language approach. Yet, both empiricists and mathematical model makers often stubbornly resist the explicit need for value judgments or even to acknowledge their necessity.

Finally, consider the ethical foundations for the newer socially oriented linguistic approach to accounting. The traditional view that language itself conditions all concepts of reality has been expanded and now includes the argument that persuasion and rational discourse themselves can support ethical systems as well as the concept of reality. Thus, the dialectic process combined with existentialistic faith in human intuition and with belief in the infallibility of the individual conscience leads to a firm foundation and reveals essential underlying values. Faith that intelligent discourse will provide ethical standards that are consistent with some broad "fundamental" values may border on Popper's dreaded "methodolatry," but in fact is no more simplistic than more traditional forms of justification. Talking ourselves into ethical beliefs may not lead to canonical virtues, but it can provide one process for arriving at social values and it is consistent with all coherence concepts of relative truth.

The newer ethical accountants are dominant in the interpersonal ethical area, but they need not deny possible objective bases for human existence. They encode (objectivize?) their own personal subjective feelings in their messages, and decoders apply their own subjective judgments to arrive at an understanding. It is not necessary to deny the concept of objectivity – in some sense or by some definition – to emphasize the importance of subjective judgment and interpersonal understanding.

Notes

1 My own experience came many decades ago in connection with the authority of universities to resist pressures from donors, legislators, students and individual faculty members to insist on their own objectives. President Robert Hutchins of the University of Chicago in the thirties argued persuasively that the very concept of university implies the authority and obligation of the institution to go beyond conflicting desires of donors and other influential groups. (A more recent case is that of Yale University's returning an endowment of some twenty million dollars rather than accede to the specific objectives of the prospective donor.) Many universities are under pressure to discontinue courses that do not "pay for themselves" and to neglect their long-accepted responsibility to expand and transmit important intellectual knowledge whether or not it will be supported by other institutions of the popular culture.

2 R. Jean Hills states: "laws of the legal variety are often referred to as examples of what scientific laws are not.... [B]oth types of laws function in the same manner.... [I]f a social entity occupies a certain status in a social group..., then the entity is expected to behave in certain ways...." *Toward a Science of Organization* (Eugene: Center for Advanced Study of Educational Administration, 1968), p. 29.

3 Students of philosophy will recognize my position here as a discourse in metaethics with no firm stand on the superiority of any particular ethical code. Kai Nielsen states: "What we shall call metaethics has been referred to as analytical ethics, critical ethics, theoretical ethics, the epistemology of ethics, the logic of ethics or ethics." And he warns: "If such a system [normative ethics] is impossible, then the task of moral philosophy is to show why this is so and to limit itself to metaethical analysis." "Ethics, Problems of," *The Encyclopedia of Philosophy*, Volume 3, Paul Edwards, editor (New York: Macmillan Publishing Co., Inc. and The Free Press, 1972), pp. 118, 119. Observe also from the same source: "The common feature of all teleological theories of ethics is the subordination of the concept of duty, right conduct, or moral obligation to the concept of the good or the humanly desirable.... [Yet even] [n]on-teleological theories... hold that the concept of duty is logically independent of the concept of good and thereby deny the necessity of justifying duties...." Robert G. Olson, *Teleological Ethics*, Volume 8, p. 88. Clearly however effective ethical codes require grounding and justification to give them authoritative status.

4 For earlier expressions see my "Ethics: General and Professional Dimensions," *Essays in Accounting Theory*, Volume V, Studies in Accounting Research 22 (Sarasota: American Accounting Association, 1985), pp. 63–77.

5 My previous positions have been ambiguous at best, but it is certainly true that I gave more attention to satisfying the master than to selecting him. For criticism of my position, see C. Edward Arrington and Anthony G. Puxty, "Accounting, Interests, and Rationality: A Communicative Relation," *Critical Perspectives on Accounting*, 1991 (2), pp. 37–8.

6 D. R. Scott, "The Basis for Accounting Principles," *The Accounting Review*, December 1941, pp. 341–9.

7 Christian fundamentalists emphasize sheer faith in the revelations given in historical texts and in early interpretations. Thomas Aquinas is a leading exemplar of the use of Aristotelian logic to deduce specific points of ethics. Some interpretations deduced just laws, usurious lending rates, unfair wage payments and just prices to restrain individual self-interest. Others inferred God's pleasure and beneficence from a healthy bottom line. For accounting treatments, see Brother LaSalle, "An Approach to Ethics," *The Accounting Review*, October 1954, pp. 687–9; and Leonard Spacek, "A Suggested Solution to the Principles Dilemma," *The Accounting Review*, April 1964, pp. 275–84.

8 Perry Mason, "The 1948 Statement of Concepts and Standards," *The Accounting Review*, April 1950, pp. 137–8.

2 Leading accountants
Ethical backgrounds

This essay was written in 1996–97 and not edited. The plan was to include: Gilman, Schmalenbach, Hatfield, May, Vatter, Kohler, Deinzer, Solomons, Spacek, Ijiri, Sterling, and Arrington, but included are John Canning, Maurice Moonitz, C. West Churchman, Richard Mattessich, Raymond Chambers, D. R. Scott, Brother LaSalle, Leonard Spacek, Tony Tinker, and the new left.

Ethics and responsibility

The relationship between ethical behavior and responsible behavior has been ambiguous. Suppose to illustrate that the ideal set of behavior has been specified from acknowledged sources so there is no question about the legitimacy of the commands, that is, for believers in God, conformance consists of following the commands and being responsible for following the commands become duties and may be equated to ethical behavior.

Unfortunately, all possible choices and trade-offs are never fully specified so that all choices worthy of the term require judgment about the appropriate rule to be applied. The selection of the appropriate rule can be called an ethical decision within the system covered by the acknowledged objectives. Even on the lowest hierarchical levels, some decisions are necessary and some freedom to choose is present. Some responsibility to the rulers is necessary and thus ethical-like decisions become necessary. These decisions are subsequent to the primary decision to accept the mandates of the commander. Thus, there may be ethical disputes even with an accepted general code of ethics due to differences in interpretations of relative importance and possible consequences. Only a homogeneous population with common interpretation and knowledge can remove this ambiguity.

Positivist – ethics

Where do professional ethics and influence appear in the accounting positivists' paradigm? Certainly, there has been no explicit mention of professional codes of ethics in their market-oriented studies. Presumably, professional attitudes – weak or strong are expressed somehow in market calculations. Professional feelings may have some influence on market actors. It is well known that government regulations sometimes influence market prices, and some regulations like rent and general price controls clearly influence market prices. Professionals do enter markets to buy and sell but there is little evidence that they participate as advocates of professional ethics. They may lobby for legislative regulation and may sometimes exert minor influence on buyers and sellers themselves. It may be possible to appeal broadly to market actors through advertising, etc., but there is little evidence of such activity.

This passive approach to professional organizations first came to my attention through March and Simon who argued essentially that businessmen made decisions based on non-accounting data, and used accounting data mostly in after-the-fact justifications.[1] The conclusion then is that accounting positivists and indeed market advocates generally allot little attention to professional codes of ethics as dynamic factors in accounting rule selection.

Agency theorists are descended from ordinary accounting positivists and carry on the market tradition. The characteristics of market participation are transferred to bureaucrats in corporate organizations. The agency man is similar to the market man (and economic man) in that he is assumed to be a greedy self-maximizer with an aversion to work and little loyalty to his organizational group. Thus, agency theorists more or less posit a sort of natural man and in the positivist tradition try to be as neutral and nonjudgmental as possible. Presumably, there is a traditional liberal sense of values in which the individual is assumed to be paramount and the organizational environment arranged by contracts to control his assumed features. It is more or less accepted that the outcomes of these contracts will not unduly favor the diffusion or concentration of power.

Positivists and responsibility ethics

The acceptance and discharge of simple responsibilities with a single host does indeed involve choices and therefore may be said to employ uncomplicated ethics. The responsible party has to make the decision to accept or not accept, but this choice can hardly be termed ethical unless other factors are at issue. Once responsibilities have been accepted, however, a continuous series of decisions to continue or to digress for alternative benefits must still be faced. After all, two parties are involved and unless the value systems are congruent, certain stresses are sure to arise. A given work load, for example, may seem reasonable and just to the employer and at the same time terribly unreasonable and unjust to many workers. In this simple case, there is no independent value system that can serve to mediate and influence decisions even though adjustments of the conflicting values is clearly necessary.

The worker may make his decision on an ethos of strict self-interest. The employer too may use a similar self-interest paradigm (with his own self-interest as paramount) and the result may be a sort of game theory strategy that accepts the results as ethical outcomes. Of course, self-interest is not a requirement for this adjustment. Christian agape may be employed in some form and all choices made in what are perceived to be the interests of the other party. In its ideal form, the ethical basis for Louis Blanc's "give according to your ability and take according to your needs" seems to be an example of an agape basis for ethics.[2] The meta-justification of particular value systems concerns us here only to the extent that in the adjustment of conflicting ethical patterns some sort of legitimization usually is employed – stark power, more generalized authority, consistency with more generally accepted ethos, etc.

The position of agency theorists is clearly self-interest. Economic theorists have long assumed that greed and self-interest are the strongest fibers of the value nets held by employers. Adam Smith recognized this set of values and set the stage for competition as a regulator to keep the results consistent with what he himself felt an economic system of values should be. The New Deal encouraged worker organizations to replace competition so that the self-interest values of workers could be more effective in getting a good and just distribution of the social output. Thus, steps were taken to mitigate the harsh consequences from conflicting self-interest systems and modify the results of the process to conform more closely with a broader ethic.

Modern accounting agency theorists make a simple extension of this conflict model to the internal workings of organizations, where the workers include all receivers of delegated authority. These agents presumably apply the same market ethical standards to actors in organizations. Thus, the resulting value systems and conflictual process are in keeping with the market process of a competitive society.

There is, however, an important difference. It is competitiveness that makes the market system an acceptable director of production and an acceptable distributor of the results. It is not so evident that the agency assumption within organizations can be depended on for legitimization of the process to meet the requirements of most social ethical patterns.

In market economies, producers compete with producers and consumers (buyers) compete with other buyers. Those in charge of delegation in organizations do not seem to be in competition in any serious sense. In fact, they may be nearer to collusion with top management through indoctrination from entrepreneurship seminars and the like. In any event, there are often not enough of them at comparable levels to bring the advantages of competition that efficient markets demand.

In similar manner, there is only limited competition among delegatees since there is some degree of freedom at all levels of management, and even among laborers there is no doubt that self-interests are at work. However, there is little evidence that competition at each of these levels can be depended upon to automatically encourage the interests of the entire organization.

In this flawed organizational environment, professional and more general ethical constraints are given little weight, and in a similar manner accounting ethics seems to be, at least for positivists, only a small (and seldom mentioned) influence on the market bidding that determines which accounting rules are finally adopted. Justification is carried over by employing market forms as an acceptable surrogate.

It should be mentioned again that a market view does not necessarily require a self-interest grounding for its ethical justification. Marx was sure that exchanging commodities at their socially necessary labor cost would serve as a satisfactory surrogate, and some societies do in fact operate on the basis of giving away all private possessions with the hope that others will do the same. Certainly, the Golden Rule contains elements of this ethos.

Canning – ethics

John Canning was an early disciple of Irving Fisher, but apparently absorbed in parts of Fisher's subjective orientation. He may have turned to more societal concerns through his later work with world food production and distribution, but in earlier years he seems to have been committed to the business economics viewpoint. His asset valuation model follows Fisher and is based on discounted expectations. The model is essentially identical to that used in cost–benefit analysis.

Canning's justification is given little attention, but it is clear that he is traditional in his ethical foundations. He is surprisingly tolerant of business practices and more tolerant than one might expect of public accountants. Canning looks to social foundations for justification and makes the usual simplifications. Businessmen follow their own self-interest with normal human limitations and look to legal sources for more specific limitations. Accountants are responsible primarily to the investor segment of the economic spectrum with the usual helping hand to managers and investors in the placement and operation of economic factors in an efficient manner. The following quotations give the general directions of his views:

> Our modern organization of business presents for our consideration the economist's view that men tend to act in their own self-interest and the legalistic view that the utmost good faith can be required and expected of those who act in a representative [fiduciary] capacity.[3]

His respect for unspecified authority – presumably governmental dicta – overcomes more broadly based human considerations; he states that

> [N]o duty of public disclosure is asserted. The accountant's duty in that regard is exactly that of any one else in receipt of a privileged communication. He is bound not to make a willing or willful disclosure unless ordered by *competent authority to do so*.[4]

However, he also betrays respect for a broader authority when he continues about the accountant:

> He is equally bound in duty to the public not to be a party to a future *consequent* harm to another person.... The accountant's duty to his client and to the public is to see to it that a minimum *future* harm is done to those not responsible for the initial prevision.[5]

Canning withholds judgment on the past performance of public accountants when he states: "But the degree of self-government now reposed in the profession, and the zeal with which the governing boards press the matter of ethical conduct...is a hopeful sign."[6]

Moonitz – ethics

Maurice Moonitz's position is difficult to assess and this attempt to do so is amateurish at best. His graduate work at Stanford brought him in contact with Canning and gave a strong bent toward economics. Canning's asset valuation model follows Fisher and is based on discounted expectations; essentially it is identical to that used in cost–benefit analysis.

Moonitz has been a strong follower of Fisher and Canning in his concept of income as changes in discounted expectations, and he devoted about a hundred pages to the concept in his highly regarded intermediate text with Staehling.[7] In this work, he regarded the use of changes in discounted expectations as the proper measure of periodic well-offness when knowledge of the future is available. In the absence of adequate knowledge, he retreated to the more "objective" methods of current market values.

Now cost–benefit analysis is used widely in public decision making as well as in the private area; Moonitz seems to have concentrated his attention on the latter. Thus, his attitudes and values were largely those of businessmen who operate in a relatively free economic environment.

Moonitz also demonstrated, along with Staehling, an unusual interest in, and apparently a respect for, the legal aspect of business intercourse. This influence may have come from Staehling as well as from his experience in a large public accounting firm. One might expect that this background would have led him, along with his colleague Perry Mason, to feel that the ethics of a society belong to legislators and legal institutions. Mason took this attitude toward ethics, but I have been unable to establish that Moonitz also took this path.

Moonitz did joint work with Littleton and was influenced by this outstanding elder statesman. Certainly Moonitz had a high regard for public accountants, and actually based ARS 1 primarily on what "accountants do."[8] Yet, this respect for what "accountants do" apparently did not last long for in his joint work in ARS 3,[9] he immediately abandons the "generally accepted" guideline for more economic and scholarly criteria.

Finally, Moonitz largely rejects the pragmatic criteria of evaluating a principle entirely by its consequences and strongly draws down the wrath of such non-pragmatists as Spacek as well of many pragmatists. While there are evidences in ARS 1 of relating functional analysis to principles formation, Moonitz seems to have been troubled by a yearning for something more fundamental. Thus, he is vague about the usefulness of the antecedent–consequence basis. Moreover, he has difficulty in specifying who are worthy recipients of any consequences. Businessmen operating in an enterprise economy certainly are among the leading candidates.

Churchman – ethics

C. West Churchman has been the resident philosopher for the management science movement and has exerted tremendous influence on Berkeley students and professors, especially Mattessich. Churchman is a follower of E. A. Singer, who in turn was a student of William James. James, it may be remembered, was interested in the "cash value" of outcomes, but apparently his highly subjective semi-religious attitude obscured the possible assignment of values to objectives and then incorporating them into a scientific decision model.

Despite occasional Platonesque reversions, Churchman was not deterred from all-out support for science and faith in the benefits of management science. Thus, it is clear that he depended heavily on scientific methodology for justification of his own view, and merits classification as both a scientist and a methodologist. Certainly, he is no primitive positivist but his own models usually accept prevailing value systems and use the "if . . . then . . ." format for specifying parameters and assigning values to objectives.

Churchman's justification of ethics beyond scientific methodology essentially concentrates on humanistic attitudes with humans a natural foundation. As I understand his position, he advances a natural instinctive tendency for all human beings to love conflict. He assumes that human beings adopt goal-directed behavior, acknowledges the influence of the social milieu (situational theories) and allows for ignorance and nonrationality that may lead to inconsistent values.

Churchman advances some interesting possibilities for assigning values. One such possibility depends on collective conscious to adopt a Platonian idea and then measures the objectives that may be arranged to reflect the nearness of expectations to these ideals. In the process, he cautions the use of disparate consciences of individuals and creates an entity known as "enlightened mankind." The latter concept apparently is close to the concept of a profession's ability to delimit and order the requirements of its commission. In each case, justification comes from acceptance of a common set of values – the consensus of humanity or some part of it.

Finally, Churchman advances an interesting alternative concept of human nature that is now gaining in popularity. This alternative is based on the assumption that the human condition contains a strong element of conflict. This assumption is essentially a natural law concept applied as an intrinsic behavioral tract, and it demands recognition in any formation of value systems and more practical codes of ethics. Thus, this concept serves as a justification for special ethical rules and also as a partial guide to forming such rules. Clearly, this approach is implicit in all arguments for the necessity of professional authority to force competing parties to conform to an accepted professional code.

Churchman like many others has considered the values of the accounting profession to be from exogenous but worthy hosts. Thus, like most professional ethicists, he looks to accounting for fulfilling responsibilities rather than for weighing various needs and developing its own value system. He differs from Mattessich and others who look to neoclassical economics for superior models in that his charge to the accounting profession is to collect and present information that will expedite the use of management science models.

Now management science models are often (but not entirely) based on self-interested semi-maximizers that approach choices in a cost–benefit way. It certainly is time for management-science models to be applied by nonprofit institutions, and thus it turns out that Churchman exhibits a strong positivist side. The methodology of science applied to whatever choices become the basis for accounting ethics. Management science itself becomes a service activity profession in the service of all persons who have certain values and characteristics. These persons have value systems and on some basis, they can make choices that affect these values. Furthermore, management science models based on cost–benefit can be applied with the function of making better decisions along some dimension of superiority. The difficulty here is an old one. Far too often, benefits run to certain individuals while the sacrifices (costs) run to others. Presumably, management scientists apply their methods to shift these beneficences and sacrifices according to the wishes of anyone who wants the fruits of scientific methods.

Thus management scientists, like accountants, must select their hosts. Accountants cannot serve all parties equally well and are not flexible enough to fill the informational needs of all. Therefore, they must develop their own values to guide their choices. Unfortunately management scientists, despite their flashing computers, cannot give individualized service to all and to this extent they too must develop a set of ethical standards to guide their decision choices.

A number of modern accountants (e.g. Arrington and Francis) have made a more general distinction between teleological and functional actions; this is similar to the distinction that I have about service organizations. Functional requires following well-defined responsibilities while teleological requires a "discernment of the good" as a value frame that aids in the weighting of interpersonal values that are to be advanced or sacrificed.[10]

Churchman recognized the limitations of teleological guidance and, as usual, posits a leader who assumes control of the weighting process. He states

> [T]he teleological basis of information policy utterly fails to solve the problem of authority, nor does it really remove the alienation of subject and observer-of-the-subject. All it does is to suggest a new question: What are the costs and benefits of trusting the master?[11]

Churchman's commitment to cost–benefit is not shattered by interpersonal values – he simply retreats to another level. Certainly, the search for "leaders" of the accounting profession in its search for professional ethics is an important question, and it often is difficult to find whether the AICPA, AAA, Securities and Exchange Commission, GAO or strong leaders like Paton perform this delicate task of constructing a value system. There may well be all sorts of costs and benefits to members of a profession if its leaders fail to understand the profession's mission or construct a miserable value system for their judgments.

From a general point of view, the process of building ethics values and finding leaders for the task is just one of the specific tasks. Someone, somewhere, somehow performs this chore, and the results cannot be equally congenial for all practicing accountants. This assumption makes the welfare of professional members paramount while the broader view should attempt to advocate a value structure that is congenial for all parties at interest. Most accounting ethicists even feel that the value interests of outside groups are dominant so long as the professional members can retain some of their own values. The problem is not solved – and indeed it is clearly impossible to value it in a definitive manner – by specifying the goals of members as dominant values, but certainly the values of members themselves are matters for consideration.

Consistency with broader ethical systems is no answer unless there is reason to privilege the independent value structure. Finally, all non-positivists must face this task. Some privilege God's will, others give precedent to genetic beliefs with the assumption that survival of the species is paramount. Absurdist writers and psychologists seem to favor survival of the existing individual over future individuals or groups. Others tie their beliefs to constructs (from observations?) of natural men, supernatural men, economic men, social animals, biological men, political men, businessmen, physical models of behavior.

Some ethicists may state that they consider the human condition to be a broad enough base, but what aspects do we observe, how are they combined, what are the conditions, and finally how can we define the humanity-old questions: What does it mean to be a human being? How do we discern the good and define a life of virtue? What (indeed) is truth?

Mattessich – ethics

Richard Mattessich may be unique in his strong duality foundation as justification of his values. His faith is in the traditional, hypothetico-deductive methodology of science and his general acceptance of the objectives of econo-accounting systems.

Most readers will be overwhelmed by his emphasis on deductive and logical systems but his contribution is much wider. The logical and deductive side of his arguments undoubtedly developed from his interest in his fellow Austrians who made up most of the Vienna circle. This group led by Carnap comprised logical positivists (later logical empiricists) who held generally that the propositions of ethics are nonsense statements devoid of any means for verification or empirical confirmation. To this group, propositions about ethics could be verified and discussed rationally in the tradition of metaethicists everywhere.

It should be pointed out that logical positivists were far from identical to Comtean positivists who now form the base for Rochester accountants. The former placed far more emphasis on the powers of deductive inference although they shared the privileging of observation statements and their rejection of metaphysical philosophy. Verification was carried on at some stage by sensual criteria although obviously not every proposition needs to be reduced to such levels. (The early Bertrand Russell held the same perilous views, which could reduce all statements to "atomic" propositions.) Logical positivists placed more emphasis on logic and mathematics to expand horizons and less on empirical observation. Thus, they emphasized the coherence theory of truth (consistent propositions and also the necessity for the system at some point to return to the mundane world of observation – a correspondence approach to truth).

Mattessich denies his characterization as a deductive theorist and points out that much of his earlier work (1964) is devoted to assembling inductive evidence by examining existing accounting systems.[12] In this area, he is similar to Moonitz and Littleton in not questioning seriously the ethical values of those who practice. In his major contri- bution (1964) he does indeed spend considerable space discussing these existing systems. In view of considerable reader misunderstand- ing, he failed to show clearly and precisely how he hoped to use these illustrations as bases for his postulates, definitions, and the like.

It is true that Mattessich took an extraordinarily broad view of accounting that rested finally on his concepts of flows, input–output, and pluralism. He gave attention to nonprofit accounting, but also included such econo-accounting areas as national-income accounting, Leontief's input–output analysis Quesnay's *tableau économique* and the usual schemes for handling international payments.

In Mattessich's earlier work (1964), he follows the logical-empiricist tradition and was not concerned directly with ethical matters. There is little more than fragmentary mention of ethics, normative models, or value judgments except for a sharp analysis of the value system implied in the field of management science. Inasmuch as he considered himself to be such a scientist, he must be held to their views. Mattessich, like all of us, must pick a host group. The commands to the accounting profession are exogenous and he does expend consid- erable effort in identifying the scientific community and the economic environment – as exemplified by management science – so these appear to be his hosts. The practical result of this selection is that ethical behavior must be analyzed in scientific terms and molded to the input requirements of management-science models.

While Mattessich has been rightly disturbed by the failure of readers to understand his inductive support for this methodology, there can be no mistake about his love affair with science, scientific methods, and management science. His early ethical views, therefore, must be inferred from his admiration of the sciences. In general, traditional sci- entists try to avoid value judgments (to the extent possible) and rely on the positivist "if…then…" formulation of antecedent–consequence relationships with ethical judgments to be specified in the second stage of analysis. The early Mattessich certainly supported this two-stage approach.

Management scientists are concerned primarily with the mechanics of decision making and, therefore, often integrate ethical and other value judgments into a one-stage model. Results are essentially simi lar in that, sooner or later, value judgments must be introduced into decisions. Unfortunately, most management scientists have done little more than to introduce objectives as parameters that need specification without stopping to consider them as decisions about values.

The later Mattessich (1984) recognizes his previous lack of concern about the value of ethical judgments and value systems. He excuses this failure by pointing out, first, that he consistently attempted to separate the formal features of his models and, second, that at the time he did not feel competent to discuss ethical matters and include them in his model-driven methodology; he stated that

> I do not claim that this will necessarily lead to a *generally satisfactory* theory, but I believe that it is the only way towards a *generally applicable* theory.... I introduced a *general* valuation assumption, thus *tolerating all specific valuation hypotheses* ....[13]

Mattessich is an unusually interesting ethical study among accountants. His extremely scholarly style and his shift in emphasis over his brilliant intellectual career makes classification easy, but discussion difficult. (Certainly, others – including Chambers – have seemed to misinterpret Mattessich in the most fundamental ways.) The following summary, therefore, may be far too simplistic and may call for severe modification.

Mattessich himself considers his chief contribution to accounting theory to be the separation of the formal theoretic model based on scientific methods from the applied aspects that deal with values and ends in view. Thus, his first step is the construction of a general "if ... then ..." model that he hopes is value-free. In the second of his two-step procedure, users may apply their own objectives as specific "ifs"; and then the general theory should point the way to appropriate "then" procedures.

This two-stage procedure is far from being a new innovation and in fact is a mainstay of positive thinking. Many modern theorists point out the impossibility of ever having value-free models and reject this approach out of hand. As usual this two-step methodology may be extremely effective when some objectives may be semi-isolated and neglected until they become important or relevant. Indeed the perfect sometimes may be the enemy of the good.

One preliminary area of confusion is the relative importance of deduction and induction in the Mattessich first step. Readers cannot be criticized for placing him in the deductive camp for he has been a leader in axiomatic construction and the deduction of formal theorems. This approach begins with an assumed natural law, termed the "duality principle," and is clearly grounded in the hypothetico-deductive methodology of science. How then can Mattessich claim to follow the inductive path?

The Mattessich claim to being an inductivist arises from his use of economic, production, and financial models as his framework and preferred analogies. These models are clearly not value-free in a strict sense and they often depend on the hidden assumptions about values that are inherent in the concepts of economic man or "production man." He clearly attempts to strip the existing economic models of their particulars and in the long tradition of phenomenologists tries to arrive at fundamental structures that are obstructed somehow from the "facade" of particulars.

A pragmatist finds the Mattessich search of economic and related literature for models puzzling at best and may conclude that he is a deductivist dedicated to the hypothetico-deductive format of science everywhere. Precisely, how does he use the economic models of Quesnay, Leontief, etc.? He seems to use them as analogies in an anecdotal form of argument. Presumably, these economic models worked in related (analogous) fields to the satisfaction of their users and presumably similar models as constructed by Mattessich will work in accounting. The objectives of these accountants would need to be close enough so similar models will provide the appropriate "thens." Observe, however, that objectives are important to model development, and objectives are far from homogeneous. A pragmatist asks again what is the warrant for assuming that a general "if... then..." model will give the appropriate "thens" for all objectives?

Clearly, Mattessich has a homogeneity problem inasmuch as every case is unique to some extent, but it is clear that it would be necessary to make some compromises and to group items along similarities that seem relevant to needs. There is reason to believe that the objectives of financial analysts and production specialists along with economists and accountants have some things in common. Yet, there must be caution here because accounting objectives are, with minor control feature exceptions, *entirely* made up of *values* and values are derived from or are closely related to objectives.

Moreover, accounting values may vary widely from economic values for the latter are limited entirely to scarcity relative to exercisable needs. Unfortunately in the past, accounting objectives have been related largely to economic scarcity values, although this relationship is not essential. It is quite possible that accountants may be asked to account for changes in and potentials for aesthetic values and any general theory should be flexible enough to allow such expansions.

In terms of more modern decision theory, Mattessich in his early years devised a model based on the models of scientific inquiry that would tend to optimize or at least point the way for accomplishment of the desires expressed in the objective function. Yet, his reliance on economic theory for his prototype means that the constituents of his model are related to economic objectives. In this sense, he is perhaps an inductivist for he claims to begin his inquiry by observing economists, their behavior, and their models. He then can claim that he generalized these behaviors through scientific maneuvers to form a "pure" scientific structure.

But the reader is left with unanswered questions. Would his model apply to noneconomic objectives? What is the need for his emphasis on postulational and deductive methods? Why did he not emphasize the torturous heuristical procedures of scientific inquiry, which by the way are logically invalid, that is, $A \supset B, B \therefore A$.

The nature of Mattessich's ethics in the early years thus remains unclear. Certainly, he identifies with economists and management scientists but these groups are far from homogeneous. It is not clear at this stage whether Mattessich identifies with capitalist or socialist economists. He does assume some sort of economic man who wishes to economize and optimize his well-being. Yet, even here the situation is obscured for his early model might (with perhaps minor modification) apply to situations where individuals wish to use resources and adopt inefficient combinations of resource allocation.[14]

Chambers – ethics

It is clear that Raymond J. Chambers accepted the ethics of free markets and was satisfied with the market outcomes. Apparently, the income distributions that result from supply and demand conditions were satisfactory, and the resulting consumer or producer "surpluses" generally were acceptable. Moreover, he seems to have been convinced that business costs include most important social costs so that entrepreneurial attempts to combine resources for minimum business costs were not seriously questioned.

Quotations given below indicate further that Chambers believed firmly in some sort of natural man whose appetites and preferences ordinarily were expressed through market results. Some critics, however, are uneasy with his conclusion that only actions and expected actions in the market were relevant to decision making.

Moreover, Chambers supports the selection of legal enactments for superior guidance in the sense that principles must be "consistent" with legal pronouncements and feels that these legal guidelines tend to reflect the desires of some broad portion of an important society. At the same time, he feels that the profession should help lead the way and perhaps fill any uncovered chinks that remain and are subject to the authority of the profession. In the following quotation he is commenting on the recommendations of ARS 7:[15]

> [T]here is a presumption [in the study] that at least the legal responsibilities of CPAs are to be recognized by them. But the phrase "which would rest upon determination by the courts" seems to imply that until the courts have ruled, and only insofar as the courts have ruled, is the law effective....
>
> The law is written for the general regulation of the relationships of all members of a society.... But the law does not...countenance the self-imposition of obligations on the members of a class...which is inconsistent with the general law...[or] on persons beyond a given class....
>
> [I]nsofar as the law is superior in effect, as representing the will of a whole society, no discussion of the responsibilities of CPAs which neglects or passes over statutorily imposed duties can be complete.[16]

That Chambers is something of a traditional utilitarian with a solid foundation in neoclassical economics is clear enough: "Means derive value from the value attached to the satisfaction of wants. Any choice involving addition to, or sacrifice of,...is based on the utility of the marginal unit...."[17]

It also is clear that Chambers is an optimizer who accepts both greed and rationality as natural conditions of man, yet he recognizes a natural noncontrollable world that must be considered by all individuals:

> Many aspects of the environment of action are fortuitous ... and uncertainty makes desirable the accumulation of means.... Because means are scarce in relation to wants, deliberate actions are chosen according to their expected capacities for yielding the greatest aggregate satisfaction of...wants....[18]

Chambers has great faith in the concept of objectivity but even objectivity is subordinated to his concept of relevance, which is his verbal symbol for the human side of accounting. His human side, in practical recommendation, ends in markets and prices, which for him are objective entities. Of the groups of humans involved he obviously favors investors, but fortunately he sees enough interconnectivity among groups to make his recommendations congenial to all groups; listen:

> The proposed theory is disciplined by *real* circumstances.... It has its own uniformity and objectivity, based on the fact that all calculation in money is intended to guide action *vis à vis* the external world of men in markets.[19]

One consistent principle is applied throughout – the relevance of information to human behaviour. Conventional accounting has no such explicit principle [?]; it therefore disregards the need of men to know where they are in objective terms and the rate at which they are approaching *real* goals.[20]

[M]onetary values assigned to events, things and transactions are at the date of assignment, the current valuation, the principles of relevance, objectivity and uniformity of valuation are satisfied.[21]

[Now:]
Prices are the only values relevant to actions in markets... [and] [e]xchange values or prices... for any person... are objective valuations.[22]

The ethics of the marketplace reign supreme in the works of Chambers and even more so in the methods of accounting empiricists and (especially) accounting positivists. The feeling that individual ends are beyond inquiry is a simple expression of positivist philosophy. (Give me the facts!) With this beginning, these accountants may argue that ethics have no place at all in the profession. Or they may admit to the need for ethics and argue that actions in the markets can serve as an acceptable surrogate for an acceptable ethical system!

The positivist view that ethics doesn't matter can be dismissed quickly, but the surrogation thesis deserves attention. The market does meld the beliefs, values, aspirations, wealth, etc. of participants. Once the value judgment that "voting by dollars" is proper – a heroic assumption – the use of market values as proxies for the individual values of worthy members of society may become acceptable. (The ethical judgments behind market values include the decision that income and wealth are distributed satisfactorily, that all participants have sufficient knowledge, and [unless one holds irrationality itself to be a value] some degree of rationality.) It may be that Samuelson's "revealed preferences" are superior to the nonoperational "consumer wants," but it is not at all clear that revealed market preferences are ethically acceptable in all societies.

D. R. Scott – ethics

Serious students of accounting theory might reasonably suppose that Scott – a friend and faithful disciple of Veblen – would be opposed to market-determined outcomes and capitalistic ethics. Such seems *not* to be the case!

As I understand Scott, he was reasonably satisfied with the distribution of income and the allocation of resources that result from a capitalistic process that incorporates *freely competitive markets.* Unfortunately, he concluded that monopolists and related restrictive practices had effectively destroyed the free competitive markets in the United States and Western Europe. The idea itself was acceptable but current institutions kept the idea from being effectively applied.

Moreover, Scott was far from optimistic about reforming the operating economic system by antitrust and regulatory means. However, neither Scott nor his mentor Veblen can be classed with modern absurdist literary figures or with members of the new-left establishment. The later disciples of despair may feel that vague solutions may exist somewhere in the human condition through anarchism and perhaps imperfectly through the application of syndicalism and related small-group organizations. Of course, absurdists make no serious attempt to find solutions and are content to point out the intolerable conditions. Both Veblen and Scott searched for and found solutions!

Veblen's solution – or improvement – for the system was to put the economic affairs in the hands of technocrats. These individuals were essentially engineers with broad social training whose inherent sense of justice and fairness to all would bring about efficient production with equitable distribution to all. A simple substitution of "politicians" or "bureaucrats" for technocrats might describe many present-day communist and even socialist recommendations.

Perhaps Scott saw accountants as embryonic technocrats. Accountants, especially cost accountants, have much in common with engineers. Moreover, accountants have an advantage over engineers for they already are concerned primarily with values while engineers give more attention to the physical aspects of production and distribution. In addition, accountants already are familiar with allocations of overhead according to benefits or services rendered. Accountants, according to Scott, were the obvious candidates for social technocrats to manage economic affairs.

The reader may now be interested in the attributes of accounting training and background that lead to this fantastic ability. After all the responsibility for devising rules that result in equitable production and distribution of material goods is a responsibility indeed. The truth of the matter is that the present process of selecting and training accountants hardly supports belief that the product will be distinguished in the ethical area!

Prospective members of the accounting profession to a large extent are self-selected, but self-selection is clearly subject to all sorts of influences. Family influences are important but do not concern us here except to point out that the early profession was composed disproportionately of members from Catholic and Jewish families. Accounting offered opportunities to become "professionals" and unlike the legal profession offered all sorts of lower- and intermediate-level job opportunities along the way.

Recruiters also have been influential but the main force here has been in the direction of making an opulent living by associating with the world of business – usually big business. This association with business and indirectly with a capitalistic economic system has been encouraged (unfortunately) in the education process. Except for limited attention to governmental needs, accounting in the past has been concerned primarily with profit-seeking institutions with attention concentrated primarily on calculation of gains and losses, and potential for future gains. The result has been an attachment to business needs and in most cases internalization of business values and ethics. It is true that limited attention was directed toward labor organizations and governmental agencies, but often this attention was focussed on reports needed for compliance. It has been only in the last two decades of the century that a public-interest emphasis has emerged. Led by such leaders as Parker, Arrington, and Tinker this movement has moved vigorously in several directions. Regardless of the variations taken, leaders owe a serious debt to the objectives of justice, fairness, and truth that form Scott's accounting principles.[23]

Brother LaSalle and Leonard Spacek – ethics

The most straightforward early statement of the use of a superior being to justify ethical guidelines was advanced by Brother LaSalle.[24] He begins his ground-breaking discussion by lamenting the use of the AICPA for both authority and justification and its use of a punitive process. He then turns to such defenses as: "[I]t's the right thing to do...[and to] the moral binding power [not only] of the code itself ... [but also] of the material contained in the code."[25] He is concerned with the content of the code and inquires about its consistency with the "Natural Law."

Brother LaSalle's structure is simple and follows the traditional dogma of the Catholic Church. His straightforward statement needs no elaboration:

> The Eternal Law is a Supreme Being's eternal plan for the universe. The Eternal Law extends to all acts and movements in

the universe.... The Eternal Law applies to all creatures, including man, and directs them in a manner proper to their nature. The Natural Law is the Eternal Law as known to man by reason. Man knows naturally, by reason, that he must do good and avoid evil.... Man recognizes an order, a plan in things.[26]

Brother LaSalle's basis for the conscience of man is clear enough, but Leonard Spacek's concept of conscience is confused with some embarrassingly pragmatic concepts. His criticism of Moonitz, for example, is straight pragmatism with means–ends association and with functional ties to ends in view.[27]

Even though Spacek was an influential public accountant, he never displayed a Littletonian attitude toward practice and its historical worth. Certainly, he was far too iconoclastic to accept practice uncritically, for his caustic eruptions about the practices of his profession are interesting and usually to the point. His firm commitment to the necessity of an auditing house "to speak with one voice" includes an autocratic insistence on uniformity and strong codes for guidance. Yet, strangely enough he railed as loudly against regulatory agencies and congressional authority.

Despite some pragmatic grounding, Spacek displays a strong need for generalization and guidance from above to support his autocratic commitment. In later years, he plaintively states that the profession must look to university theorists rather than practitioners for guidance even though he often had castigated professors for their ability to speak on "principles" without the restraints imposed by public practice. In view of his upper-directed beliefs, this position is roughly equivalent to holding that professors are more competent to vulgarize the Thomist Eternal Law than practitioners – a complete reversal of his early position.

This characterization may seem to be far too simplistic, but listen to some of Spacek's own statements of belief:

> [A] principle unsupported by sound reasoning is nothing more than any arbitrary rule.... [To establish accounting principles] will require initiative.... To develop *initiative*, we need only listen to our conscience. This will inevitably lead us to assume our proper responsibility.[28]

This quotation illustrates several facets of Spacek's ethical foundation and its epistemological grounding. First his use of the undefined phrase "sound reasoning" displays a deep faith in rationality and suggests the possibility of determining a Natural Law from God's Eternal Law. In this faith he follows Thomas Aquinas' position that was derived from the application of Aristotle's rationality, then he goes to orthodox Catholic dogma. The use of the adjective "sound," however, shows a disposition to use semantic supports. Presumably, "sound" means any reasoning consistent with Aristotelian logic.

Spacek introduces an interesting variable in the form of initiative. Precisely how initiative – either in an individual or in a profession – is derived from sound reasoning is not clear. But even less clear is the process of getting conscience from initiative. His use of conscience of course is not novel, and follows the teachings of both Natural Law advocates and those who somehow construct a concept of humanity and its "natural" human condition. Clearly it also is consistent with the spiritual basis for ethical activity.

Tinker and new-left ethics

Tony Tinker, and perhaps others, apparently favor a variation of the postulated economic man to a subspecies that might be termed the Marxist man or at least a socialist man. While this modification seems to vary little from the assumption of a neoclassical economic man, the difference in fact is enormous. Most Marxists reject the use of a price system for melding differing value systems. Some have gotten involved in a mystical mission of socially necessary labor units with the implication that these labor units are acceptable measures of economic values and (like market advocates) that economic values are of prime importance.

Constant references to materiality by Marxists might seem to indicate some physical basis (ala Sterling) for grounding their values, but materiality actually has little to do with Marxist values. In a similar sense, their emphasis on historical matters might lead one to associate them with Littleton. There is little or no basis for this identification. Historical necessity for the faithful is a method for supporting belief in the inevitability of Marxist progress. In turn this interest in progress as an important value would seem to be in tune with Dewey's faith. While the early Dewey was deeply interested in Hegel and his concept of dialectic necessity, Dewey so far as I know, fully accepted the necessity for a directional vector of progress that inevitably led to a supreme value system. Dewey seems to have arrived at his acceptance of democratic values through prior acceptance of some human characteristics and needs.

Tinker seems to be nearer to the more general – nonscientific – side of the spectrum. He is deeply concerned with the human condition and the vulnerability of its institutions. In one sense, he is trying to construct a field of virtues and discern the "good" for all humanity. Unfortunately to many, he relies far too heavily on Marxist sociology and economics to arrive at his value system. Some critics may want to place him with the methodologists, since he relies so much on Marxist methods of inquiry.

We turn now to some attitudes of the new left toward value. Unfortunately, this group is so broad that it often includes nihilists, individualists, ethnologists, and in most cases an absurd approach combined with a syndicalist emphasis on the individual. This movement may be characterized by its extreme emphasis on the individual and his specific value systems and its extreme antagonism to social institutions of all kinds except their own. With such a worldview, professional ethics are relatively unimportant except as it conflicts with individual, do-my-own-thing values. The hostility to any controlling institutions means that their feelings of social responsibility are weak.

The new-left movement already has had some influence on accounting ethics and practices. General purpose statements (and objectives) are downgraded in favor of special reports for individual needs. The concept of income as a desirable measure of aggregate performance is sometimes trashed. Moreover, the control devices such as standard cost accounting, budgeted revenues, and target profit planning often are considered to be stifling influences on individuals, and attempts to "socialize" their behavior. The reduction of such devices clearly makes the concept of responsibility more difficult to measure and implement. Internal controls are a clear-cut invasion of privacy and inhibitors of individual freedom. In the extreme, this group approaches the level of absurd literature with: "My ethics are as good as yours," "Don't play God," and the like. In absurd literature, compassion for the individual is simply lacking with no goals, objectives, or values to guide individual action. New-left accountants may be even more despair ridden for they see some individuals as not just compassionless but as outright enemies who try to control individuals in their own selfish interests.

In the new-left view most institutions are per se bad for they try to control and inhibit individual behavior. The value systems of our national government, the various states, countries, cities, and universities are therefore suspect. Even disdained accountants attack themselves as spies and enforcers for these institutions and especially to the arch manipulators – businessmen – and do irreparable harm to individuals. Modern accounting dissidents usually accept the values of an assumed humanity and wish to guide accounting ethics toward the values of these human (or superhuman) beings. It is not clear that an ardent disciple of the new left would move toward any generalized scheme of human ethics. Values to the people! Individual people!

Exogenous commanders in accounting

Churchman, the resident philosopher of the management science group, Mattessich, an original thinker in accounting and perhaps many others have assumed that a master group outside the accounting profession is acknowledged so that the objectives of this group become dominant, akin to religious morals. Accounting ethics then is closely related to responsibility and requires the adoption of a set of rules of behavior whose probable consequences further these exogenous objectives. In pragmatic terms, the ends in view are specified and acceptable (deferred) accounting rules become sub-objectives that operate as *means*, for example, intermediate ends.

Thus, if there is agreement about who is commander and his objectives, the difficulty in selecting ethical behaviors is reduced. The problem thus is one of hierarchy and the subdivision of goals into appropriate actions. These actions may be semantically related to responsibility and responsible actions. Unfortunately, selection of the commander is not so simple and with pluralism the ethical problem becomes broader than one of responsible behavior: Responsible to whom? It is at this point that professional ethics becomes acute.

The problem for the accounting profession is far from being that simple, for the commander is not clear-cut and numerous parties have a legitimate claim on the output of the accounting process. The importance of these claims must be evaluated and ordered before deriving ethical standards. Decisions require furthering the interests of some parties and obstructing the interests of others. Only with homogeneous commanders would the interests of all be identical and all rules consistent. This condition leads to a professional ethics that extends beyond the usual domain of responsibility. (Responsible to the dominant group.)

It is not quite accurate to say that a profession develops its conscience (Garden of Eden) and becomes aware of the necessity for professional ethics at this point, for even with a homogeneous commander the need to weigh the consequences of failure to accept responsibilities is present.

It is common to refer to a code of professional ethics as supplementary to the laws and statutes that apply generally but fail to cover specific points. This view may have heuristic and even explanatory value, but it applies equally well to situations that involve a unified commander with homogeneous objectives and to those with diverse (nonhomogeneous) goals.

Some comments on this view may be in order. First the profession must adapt to existing laws, but it has some freedom as to which claims and legal rulings it chooses to follow. Thus, professional leaders must interpret their commission from society and decide which laws are appropriate and also which chinks need to be filled. Yet, even here there is a glitch for society that may informally commission the auditing profession to vouch for management's representations and also to see that enterprise resources are not squandered but are directed to the accomplishment of enterprise goals. There may be a chain of statutes covering these functions but there remains an area of discretion for the profession in the area of behaviors necessary to perform the functions as well as the need to decide the nature of the functions and to interpret the statutes that cover it.

In the case of homogeneous goals, these interpretations may be in terms of simple agency and other hierarchical statutes and a filling in of the details necessary for carrying on the work. To some extent in the moral domain, these are the specifics of individual behavior necessary to carry out the moral code from above. In this case, there is a set of laws that needs to be interpreted and reinterpreted in terms of the specifics of cultural possibilities.

The case involving different parties and diverse needs is more interesting. It is at this point that simple functional is replaced with teleology, a broader view that involves seeking the common good that requires recognition of the "virtues" and replaces the simpler rule of accepting responsibility. It is interesting that most, if not all, institutions – not just service professions – sooner or later reach this stage of maturity. Public universities, for an important related illustration, clearly owe some allegiance to the taxpayers that shell out operating funds in early stages and may indeed have to answer to *legislators* for offering esoteric courses that cannot possibly meet the often expressed requirements that each course pay for itself or meet a partial standard.

At a later stage of development the very term "university" takes on defining properties and the institution develops an inner dynamic of its own. Historically, this dynamic supports the more general mission of preserving the intellectual heritage and expanding such activity as well as transmitting it. Research in intellectual activities becomes a defining property and to sponsor such research and to disseminate the results becomes a requirement of those institutions that wish to call themselves universities. In many areas, universities along with some research foundations become the only institutions that support rigorous investigation of much of the materials covered in the field of humanities if not the entire field of liberal arts.

Notes

1 See James G. March and Herbert A. Simon, *Organizations* (New York: John Wiley & Sons, Inc., 1958), pp. 161–2.

2 *Editors' Note:* Carl is likely referring to Louis Blanc (1811–62), a French historian whose works include a history of the French Revolution. A similar reference to the idea of "from each according" is made in Essay 1 of Volume 5 of Carl's *Essays in Accounting Theory*. Carl provided no specific reference there either with respect to where he obtained this insight.

3 John B. Canning, *The Economics of Accountancy* (New York: The Ronald Press Company, 1929), p. 326.

4 Ibid., p. 249 (emphasis added).

5 Ibid., pp. 249–50.

6 Ibid., p. 326.

7 Maurice Moonitz and Charles C. Staehling, *Accounting: An Analysis of its Problems*, Volume I (Brooklyn: The Foundation Press, Inc., 1952), pp. 107–212.

8 Maurice Moonitz, *The Basic Postulates of Accounting*, Accounting Research Study No. 1 (New York: AICPA, 1961).

9 Robert T. Sprouse and Maurice Moonitz. *A Tentative Set of Broad Accounting Principles for Business Enterprises*, Accounting Research Study No. 3 (New York: AICPA, 1962).

10 The relevant statement is: "Teleological action requires hermeneutical discernment of the *good* of an action, and that discernment determines *how* action proceeds.... Functional action is involuntary and non-teleological – it does not involve hermeneutical work." C. Edward Arrington and Jere R. Francis, "Accounting and the Labor of Text Production: Some Thoughts on the Hermeneutics of Paul Ricoueur," Working Paper, Project on Rhetoric of Inquiry, The University of Iowa, Iowa City, 1989, p. 63. The authors revised this paper and published it without the statement presented above under the title: "Giving Economic Accounts: Accounting As Cultural Practice," *Accounting, Organizations and Society*, 2/3, 1993, pp. 107–24.

11 C. West Churchman, *The Design of Inquiring Systems: Basic Concepts of Systems and Organization* (New York: Basic Books, Inc., Publishers, 1971), p. 164.

12 Citations to the two works by Richard Mattessich are *Modern Accounting Research: History, Survey, and Guide*, Research Monograph 7 (Vancouver: The Canadian Certified General Accountants' Research Foundation, 1984); and *Accounting and Analytical Methods: Measurement and Projection of Income and Wealth in the Micro- and Macro-Economy* (Homewood: Richard D. Irwin, Inc., 1964).

13 Richard Mattessich, "On the Evolution of Theory Construction in Accounting: A Personal Account," *Modern Accounting Research: History,*

Survey, and Guide, Research Monograph 7 (Vancouver: The Canadian Certified General Accountants' Research Foundation, 1984), p. 34.

14 For Richard Mattessich's own assessment of his efforts and accomplishments, see his *Foundational Research in Accounting: Professional Memoirs and Beyond* (Tokyo: Chuo University Press, 1995).

15 Paul Grady, *Inventory of Generally Accepted Accounting Principles for Business Enterprises*, Accounting Research Study No. 7 (New York: AICPA, 1965).

16 R. J. Chambers, "A Matter of Principle," *The Accounting Review*, July 1966, p. 444; reprinted in R. J. Chambers, *Accounting Finance and Management* (Sydney: Arthur Andersen & Co., 1969), pp. 243–4.

17 R. J. Chambers, *Accounting Finance and Management* (Sydney: Arthur Andersen & Co., 1969), p. 509.

18 Ibid., p. 510.

19 Ibid., p. 516 (emphasis added).

20 Ibid., p. 515 (emphasis added).

21 Ibid., p. 514.

22 Ibid., pp. 510–11.

23 D. R. Scott, "The Basis for Accounting Principles," *The Accounting Review*, December 1941, pp. 341–9.

24 Brother LaSalle, "An Approach to Ethics," *The Accounting Review*, October 1954, pp. 687–9.

25 Ibid., p. 687.

26 Ibid., p. 688.

27 See Maurice Moonitz, *The Basic Postulates of Accounting*, Accounting Research Study No. 1 (New York: AICPA, 1961), pp. 56–7.

28 Leonard Spacek, "A Suggested Solution to the Principles Dilemma," *The Accounting Review*, April 1964, pp. 279, 283. This rambling discourse begins with sharp criticism of professional practices, but also shows his budding efforts to find a basis for more general ethical guidelines.

3 Addendum
Different views of natural man

What sort of man is the traditional natural man? What about primitive man? Christian man? A superman with a will to control the world? It is dangerous to assume that learned men are more likely to arrive at consensus. More consensus may exist among the uneducated whose belief often is based on myth, tradition, supernatural religions, and the like.

The most common cleavage is between man as compassionate, sweet, and caring at one extreme; and as a depraved, untrustworthy animal at the other. Of course, genuinely enlightened people usually will take a middle view that allows for both good and bad behavior, but unfortunately the extremes often are presented to bolster untenable arguments. Attitudes toward this cleavage are extremely important in all branches of social study. They certainly are paramount in political science where concern often is with the scope and legitimacy of political power. Clearly, this division is present from the very beginning in discussions of worker–employer relations and is at the center of the tops-down, bottoms-up controversy. Therapists, analysts, and run-of-the-mill psychologists face the problem before selecting treatment for the disturbed. Economists make all sorts of weird assumptions about their created entities and their recommendations for interpersonal controls.

Finally, accountants – especially auditors – are faced immediately with the need for assumptions about the nature of man and with the necessity to arrange controls when conflicts arise. Accountabilities, responsibilities, equities, entities, disclosure necessities, measuring techniques, reporting methods, and the selection of accounts to represent areas of interest – indeed the whole structure is based on definite conceptions of man and what it means to be a human being.[1]

Internal controls, for example, presuppose a man who is acquisitive, honest (at least up to thirty dollars), intelligent enough to cover up simple defalcations, antisocial enough to resist sharing his needs and plans with possible colluders. Negative controls usually are employed first. The accounting man is interested in pleasing those in his organization, but is deeply concerned about being caught and subjected to the consequences of fraud and defalcation. The psychology here is primitive at best and depends largely on the deterrent effect of fear rather than to the cooperative spirit of fellowship. In effect, the possible defector is either too dumb to see the collusive path to success or too socially timid to approach others and go forward with his plans. Notice also that his sense of loyalty to the firm is extremely weak so that his group socialization is suspect. A selfish what's-in-it-for-me attitude is presumed although it is not usually as pervasive as in the agency-contracting man of modern agency paradigms.

Internal controls also assume that the clerical (no-funds handling member) displays different characteristics. First, he has been subjected to clerical professionalism which instilled respect for honesty and the worthiness of his tasks and for written records. Interesting psychological assumptions lie behind the physical separation of clerical workers from those who handle the resources. Thus, the clerical members of the internal-control cycle are indoctrinated to be relatively unsocial and have little intercourse with physical types. Thus, they are encouraged to be introverted or at least isolationist with low thresholds for moving around. Certainly, bookkeepers and clerks are not above suspicion and require at least minimal socialization.

The auditor in turn is trained to be suspicious and to develop a low appraisal of human nature. He is professionalized into believing that those in organizations, including managers, have relatively low thresholds for honesty and integrity. Worse, he also suspects customers, visitors, and all others who might come into contact with an organization and its resources. It may not be quite true that he expects to find "slime under every rock," but he certainly develops a low opinion of natural man and his natural inclinations. Fortunately, it is not necessary to believe that all men lean to depravity, for controls become necessary even if only a few are so inclined.

Consider now the accounting profession's espousal of conservatism to resist a supposed tendency to "puff" one's status and observe the financial officer's assumption about investor and entrepreneur risk. Reflect also on attitudes about the inclinations of workers and consumers. In a broader realm, consider legal rules of evidence and self-interest testimony, the Judeo-Christian doctrine of original sin and Marxist expectations when capitalistic shackles have been removed. Even educators are divided on the relative importance of heredity and the limits of educatability, and their tentative approach to improving learning conditions.

The Christian religions generally accept the bad-guy approach to human nature and make innumerable references to original sin and the pitiful plight of man since curiosity overcame Adam and Eve. Christian fundamentalists are genuinely appalled by the negative features of human nature and often combine them with personification under one easy-to-identify responsible culprit. Preachers often seem to enjoy their weekly castigation of the constructed personification. To overcome these bad features and to develop the embryonic seeds of goodness, a benign authority is developed with the power to reward those who develop good characteristics and punish the bad. Positive reinforcement and negative deterrents are combined with rewards and punishments of heroic magnitude.

It often has been asserted that communism has an optimistic ethical edge over Christianity by assuming that man's nature is benign but has been corrupted by the wicked institutions of capitalism. Once these evil influences have been removed, it is assumed that the essential goodness of man's nature will come to the surface and all will be well. In the communist case, the culprit is definite and easily identified but (so far) difficult to remove. For intellectuals, the identification of original sin (without logical justification) may be more difficult to accept than the identification of greedy capitalistic institutions as the culprit.

The effects of original sin cannot be removed, but they can be mitigated with constant struggle by following Christian doctrine. The effects of capitalist institutions are no less real but they too may be removed by revolution and establishment of Marxist methods. It is not clear whether the installation of Marxist institutions removes the continuing struggle with the capitalist devil but Marx' commitment to the dialectic implies a continuing struggle to improve the direction of the syntheses until some sort of ideal is reached – a kingdom of Marxist men on earth!

It should be noted that a Marxist-like split preceded the communist program by several centuries. Many Christians of the enlightenment believed that the condition of mankind would automatically "progress" to better and better things if the heavy-handed institutions of the Catholic Church could be removed.

The Luther attempt at reformation expanded, overflowed the boundaries of church squabbles and became the general voice of the enlightenment. In this expansion, religion itself became the enemy that opposed all efforts to improve the human condition. Faith in mankind's goodness became the centerpiece; and if left alone, mankind would inevitably (with perhaps some help from humanist intellectualism) progress toward a better life. In later days, this attitude has become widespread and has to some extent become the belief support for John Dewey and his recommendations for education.

Examples of these conflicting assumptions about the nature of man are numerous in the study of political leaders. Niccolò Machiavelli (*The Prince*) certainly took a negative view and advocated stern governmental controls. Thomas Hobbes (*Leviathan*) expected more or less ruthless leaders to set acceptable social norms. Adam Smith, as a good child of the enlightenment, expected an invisible hand to alleviate the obvious ills of unrestricted greed. Darwin and subsequent advocates of Social Darwinism emphasized the urge for survival; and, in a manner reminiscent of Smith, held that the urges for survival might somehow lead to a degree of cooperation. It is this belief that merits his inclusion in the optimistic camp for his competition tends to foster the cooperation necessary for social living. It also is interesting to note that the philosopher Henri Bergson, despite his enthusiastic *élan vital*, had serious doubts about the ability of man's reason and compassion to control his innate predatory nature.

Optimistic political and economic leaders were children of the enlightenment, but a millennium or so before, Cicero asserted that leaders could and should rule by voluntary approval, and not by crass and repressive means. John Locke is no doubt the prime exemplar of the idealist and optimistic view. With the help of man's inherent reasonableness, governmental controls could be shaped by public opinion and the government could be reduced to little more than a bundle of pragmatic practices for administration. Certainly, the American founding fathers were firm believers in the Lockean dogma.

The influence of the enlightenment has been so great in America and Dewey's educational view has been so dominant that most Americans hardly realize that an opposing legitimate view exists. Inasmuch as much of the world is and has been governed by despots – often of the most vicious kind – this optimistic view certainly has shown amazing vitality.

In the area of management, the nature-of-man controversy took the form of tops-down, bottoms-up attitudes. The traditional pessimistic view was the basis for management philosophy of the early twentieth century and was advocated by Taylor, Urwick, and a host of other forceful managers and engineers. In accounting and auditing, this view meant that reports and monitoring efforts were about inferiors made to superiors. Clearly, such efforts relate to responsibilities and are directed to those who have the power to force conformance with group goals.

The optimistic view is represented by Douglas McGregor, Elton Mayo, Chris Argyris, and many others. Their position views each level of employee as a center with ideas of worth that should be presented to superiors and others in the firm. In some cases, both optimism and pessimism are present with some leaders looking at man's values as largely environmentally determined and others relating them to a dominant hereditary base. Warren Bennis, a member of the modern group, apparently holds with Marx-like inevitability that there will be constant progress toward decentralization and away from bureaucratism because of the increasing force of technology and the need for at least semi-professionalism and understanding at all levels.

The modern contracting-agency view is an extreme version of the usual basis for capitalistic economic organization. Each member of an organization is assumed to be a business-like, self-maximizer bent on furthering his own private interests. He exercises an extreme form of individualism where the modern-day ethic of "what's in it for me" is supreme. Members of organizations apparently feel no loyalty to related individuals or groups and fail to internalize organizational values beyond the amounts necessary to further individual objectives. It is true that in the general ethical environment, organizational and professional values influence the goals of each individual. However, there is little or no emphasis on professionalism and allegiance to professional codes of ethics or to Christian *agape*, which gives little consideration to personal gain. Clearly, the agency framework takes a dim view of the human condition and a negative assessment of human nature. Moreover, it establishes no overt need to improve the situation; rather than trying to change human nature, its advocates take a positivist turn and attempt to arrange human tasks and relationships so that all can go their own selfish ways and yet accomplish enough so that all are partially satisfied. Apparently, each agent at each contracting level is satisfied with his own working arrangements that afford opportunities to optimize rewards such as leisure, on the job power, prestige, and monetary compensation.

Often bottoms-up and agency literatures fail to emphasize the motivation for each agent to develop new methods and procedures that will benefit the organization. Presumably, each employee feels that by passing along good ideas to those above, he will somehow improve his own personal position. There are glaring dysfunctional forces at work here, and a major problem of management is to create the feeling that by developing *and passing on* new ideas, the original worker also will profit. Even so, there always is a tendency for agents to fail to disclose ideas that harm his own personal ambitions.

Perhaps the rewards may be large enough to overcome this bias from selfishness or perhaps each member can be indoctrinated to accept professionalism and the goals of the organization. In any case, we are back to the age-old problem of buying conformance or rearranging the selfish nature inherent in the human condition. Bottoms-up managers, therefore, show some optimism and hope that they can improve human nature or at least rearrange the conditions of work so that chances for goal identification and goal congruence are increased. Thus, the human nature assumed by bottoms-up theory is not identical with the nature assumed by agency-contracting theorists.

The agency-contracting paradigm in accounting and the emergence of strong support for bottoms-up attitudes present that basis for some interesting asides. It may or may not follow that more responsibility at all levels in an organization will lead to more selfish attitudes and less loyalty to the organization. This latter group in accounting feel that – for some reason – employees at all levels develop a grasping, self-centered attitude toward any new idea that may crop up. They seem to presume that the motivation for new ideas is derived largely from self-interest and very little from a desire to further the interests of the organization. This question is debatable for it may be that more freedom encourages a deeper group identification and less self-interest. In any event, accountants may face a new challenge at this point. A demand may develop for accounting reports that help individuals at all levels to attain their own personal goals. Such a conclusion is not foregone because accountants might assume that internalization of firm values will be enough for employees at lower levels to take the side of the organization. It may be argued that the scope of responsibility accounting should be broadened to account for the contributions made by employees at all levels – whether the motivation is self-centered or directly for the benefit of the organization. At the other extreme, it may be argued that accounting should be decentralized with special reports for each employee to indicate how well his own greedy efforts are succeeding. Decentralized well-offness (profit) accounting might then be carried to the ultimate: a separate report for each employee's well-being along with all sorts of combinations that may or may not reach to the top of the entire organization.

Thus, accountants might consider a special vector that reports on the accomplishment of separate objectives of each individual and each group or combination. A period's progress, for example, might be reported from the viewpoint of each intermediate or low level employee along with progress toward the different objectives of sections, groups, divisions, and the entire business. The assumption of rational maximization of each member in the agency-contracting cycle may make the mathematical manipulations easier, but so far it is not clear how these efforts are influenced by personal goals as opposed to firm loyalty, and appropriate accounting techniques still seem to be in doubt.

Turn now to the more traditional accounting views and do not be surprised that these views usually are in line with those of industrial managers. From the accounting perspective, mankind is definitely on the negative side. Accountants have unequalled chances to observe owners and entrepreneurs under stress, and note their reactions to financial and other stresses. The accountant's picture is somewhere between the extremes set by those who argue that businessmen are without ethics and others who see nothing wrong with actions that meet the narrow test of legality. There is no doubt that a society that measures success largely in terms of wealth tends to sharpen the aggressive and selfish tendencies in man and sanctions some actions that seem unreasonable to others. At the same time, there can be little doubt that the self-interest motive is a tremendous factor in producing goods and services efficiently. Yet, the assumption that all men are bad and businessmen are among the worst is certainly not an accounting observation. Most businessmen have been influenced by institutions of their societies and accept all sorts of constraints on their goals as legitimate. This balance is indeed delicate and accountants have an excellent opportunity to observe it in dynamic action.

In the financial area, the most obvious evidence of accounting's negative view is in the flawed but time-honored area of conservatism. While this view may have numerous alternative defenses, a common one is related to an assumed tendency of managers (and others in charge) to stress their successes, play down their failures, and generally slant their reports to further their own interests. To my knowledge no scientific (statistically significant) support has been deduced to support this position, but centuries of observational and anecdotal evidence support this belief. While it is true that all vital and useful knowledge cannot be shown to be statistically significant, other less formal support usually can be found. Lawyers are aware of the best-foot-forward tendency in giving depositions and other evidence. Voters do not expect their candidates to emphasize their negative features and accomplishments. Men of the cloth are well aware of the possibility of under-stated confessions as well as public statements. Management's representations may indeed require support from independent operators.

Auditors are in an excellent position to observe human beings under stress, and their overall judgment tends toward a negative assessment of human beings engaged in business and governmental affairs. The entire function of the profession is to prevent and bring to light various nonfunctional activities by subordinates and any misrepresentation of pertinent results. In this respect, the profession may be nearer to psychology than to the doctrines of traditional accounting. Certainly, a major function is to ferret out and report dysfunctional activities; but in recent years, emphasis has shifted to the prevention of such activities. Misrepresentations may be due to error, and poor handling of resources may be due to sloppy routines. Certainly, such deviations should be discovered and reported so that they may be corrected or eliminated. In addition, any tendency toward self-interest activities must be identified and circumvented. Whether or not such activities are fraudulent depends, of course, on the appropriate laws governing fraud. In any case, auditors must enlarge their operations to include not only fraud but also to help discover misrepresentations which are not entirely the result of error, yet do not meet the technical definition of fraud. If one is to accept the inherent properties of an agency-contracting man, auditing must apply to all levels and perhaps be expanded to disclose the overall cost to the organization of dysfunction from individual self-interest and failure to internalize organizational goals.

Cost accountants often are divided, but traditionally they have followed the old tops-down approach to the control of subordinates who have interests of their own that sometimes prevent internalization of group objectives. The older approach was to use variances to locate both satisfactory and trouble spots in an organization, to apply direct pressure on erring responsibility centers, and unfortunately to a lesser degree, apply positive reinforcement to those with favorable variances. Fear of red variances was the direct outgrowth of fear of reprimand or job separation.

Some cost accountants have taken a more optimistic view of the human condition so that variances are less used as a weapon for controlling recalcitrant employees. This view looks at standards and variances as devices for planning and coordinating activities. These accountants and managers condemn the use of standards and variances as figurative clubs and some even counsel withholding the results from the employees affected. These are certainly alternative motivating devices. Alternative methods are advocated by those who fear that feedback of actual results helps employees adjust their own aspiration levels and gives them information about what the firm expects from them. For the last half century, most cost accountants have taken the latter view. Modern management theorists no doubt feel that accountants have been slow to adapt. Accountants are expected to take care of the details of setting standards, measuring deviations, and the like; and indeed have been slow to take avant garde positions on the psychological niceties of motivation, control, and deterrence. Perhaps this tardiness should be corrected and the order reversed.

The entity theory – so forcefully advocated by Paton and his disciples – was a stumbling block for accounting for a diversity of interests and objectives. The older proprietorship approach emphasized the importance of owners and looked at investors, workers, governmental agencies, and the like as little more than contributors to the environment who must be bought off or satisfied in some way. Unfortunately, this approach has recently resurfaced in the field of corporate finance with the chief objective of management limited more or less to "enhancing residual (corporate) value." At first sight, the entity theory looks as if it restricts the accounting outlook to a narrow concept of an organization, but such was not the intent of Paton and his followers. It is true that investors still can view managers as if they were economic goods to be distributed according to the marginal principle and expect accountants to monitor and report on their successes and failures. A successful entity (with a healthy residual value) usually benefits all members of an organization including workers, tax collecting agencies, suppliers, and customers; but the entity theory, at least in the early Paton version, did give more than overall entity success measures. For example, it disclosed how well bond holders were being covered and gave information for preferred stockholders. Further, information on the contributions of product and marketing divisions and on worker efficiency could easily be incorporated into the entity format. The resulting reports were not only useful in controlling various facets of the business, but they were also useful in planning and coordinating activities.

Note

1 The objective here is not to address the question of the relative importance of environment, culture, etc. as opposed to innate drives, yens, dispositions, instincts, traits, and the like. Clearly, however, this subject is of immense interest to accountants who are unavoidably interested in possibilities for training, indoctrinating, and educating those who construct the web and those who might be caught in its snares. I have been greatly influenced in this area by "Human Relations and the Nature of Man," by Henry P. Knowles and Borge O. Saxberg, *Harvard Business Review*, March–April 1967, pp. 22 ff.

4 Hermeneutics and communication theory[1]

The similarities between hermeneutics and current information theory are obvious yet many fail to see the vital differences. It is important to note in advance that the early Shannon–Weaver[2] research is not concerned with human communication except in a remote technical way. In their structural format, an individual possesses a definite, more or less unambiguous, message that he must encode in some manner for transmission. In various random and nonrandom ways noise enters the system through such naturalistic creations as atmospheric conditions, electrical eccentricity, human error, or some technological breakdown. The message that emerges from the transmission is obscured or in some way not identical to the message encoded. The message available to the receiver, therefore, is different from the message sent by the initiating party.

At this point, it is common to distinguish between information and communication, and to bring individuals into the expansion. Until this point, the emphasis is on the technical determination of some idealized mechanical message and its distortions. This emphasis on the transmission phase is far too limited and too simplistic for hermeneuts, for transmission imperfections are only one kind of uncertainties and ambiguities found in human communication.

In hermeneutics personal and individual aspects of communication are emphasized. For example, the sender is never quite sure about the structure of the message that will create the desired effect on the receiver. Thus, in a game-like situation he must anticipate the reactions of probable receivers and try to construct his message as a kind of metaphor so that after surviving possible distortions in transmission something near his intended meaning will be received and incorporated in the receiver's decisions and actions. Thus, interdependence must be considered and the original message must be constructed to include probabilistic and unknown perils of transmission as well as a wide range of possible interpretations. Alienation is unavoidable because the sender is "foreign" to all possible receivers and to the operators who make the transmission. Certainly, uncertainties face each party, and additional help from probability theory is absolutely necessary.

Hermeneuts select a process of transmission – a language – to transmit their own ambiguous messages. This language, with or without electrical and mechanical difficulties, is clearly polysematic and ambiguous in both its terms and modes. Many traditional accountants seem to believe that the encoding language is precise and that the encoding process (making the appropriate entries) is without serious error. Ambiguities, except for errors in recording, are added later by poor summarization, presentation, and interpretation. A part of this difficulty is that accountants have not carefully examined the nature of a transaction, and the unambiguous nature of the accounting language of debits and credits. In fact, the decision about what events are to be selected to serve as transactions is open and extremely difficult. Which events *are* critical? What aspects of the selected events are to be encoded? At what amounts?

These problems of event recognition deserve more attention. The literature of critical-event analysis has been sterile and has avoided the fundamental need to *decide* which of the myriad of events in the history of an enterprise are to be considered critical and which are not. This decision requires the formulation of selection rules, and useful rules require value judgments. The use of "fundamental" flows as the rule is sterile and leads to misplaced emphasis. Which flows *are* fundamental to our objectives? Which flows are of little or no consequence for the task at hand? (Forget for the moment that the term flow is a metaphor selected from physics and has little similarity to the discrete changes in well-being that are of concern to accounting.) Clearly, no royal road or "fundamental" analogy will help here. Why are some events critical and others not? Why are some flows more *fundamental* than others? Why are some assumptions more *basic* than others? There are no easy answers, but attention must be directed to the needs of worthy users and to estimates of the ability of expected consequences to fulfill these needs. It is not so much that accounting tradition has been wrong. The benefits from the profession are obvious. The problem is that while accountants do pretty well at the actual task of selecting rules to recognize transactions, they pay little attention to justifying and analyzing the process. Simplistic assertions about "basic assumptions," "critical events," and "fundamental flows" without analysis are indications of an immature profession.

Professional literature is strewn with equally vacuous assertions about the dimensions of an event to be encoded and transmitted. Except for some recent work by Ijiri,[3] the profession has pretty much decided to emphasize only two dimensions of a transaction (i.e. the status and changes in wealth on the one side, and the status of and changes in equity claims on the resources of an entity). While the wealth–equity dimensions form the basis for traditional double-entry bookkeeping, accountants in fact monitor and report many other types of information. It may indeed be possible to keep pseudo double-entry books with only one asset account and one equity account, but the very fact that many different accounts are used to provide more detail indicates the expanded need for information.

For some types of cost accounting and auditing a classification based on responsibilities accepted and responsibilities fulfilled may be more useful than the traditional wealth orientation although some accountants (e.g. Moonitz) are reluctant to call such activities double-entry. Furthermore, some disclosures may be within the framework through reserves, appropriations, memo entries, explanatory notes, supplementary expansions, and the like. Emphasis often is added by placement in the statement, by the order of the presentation, through bold-faced type and indentations. Finally, various internal control documents and procedures may not be essential to a proper definition of double-entry, but they clearly form a part of the accounting task.

This is not the place to speculate about or construct systems that account for esthetics, costs to future generations, environmental deterioration, and ethics generally. But it is true that many important financial and operational characteristics may be handled only as supplementary additions to double-entry activities and many, like rates of progress to goals, are now handled by using double-entry data with a wide range of operations from other disciplines. Many modern accountants are moving toward a second-derivative system of accounts that provides for measuring and reporting the rate of progress toward goals – a type of triple entry.

In any case, the encoder may have encountered tremendous uncertainties before he is ready to objectivize and transmit his message. These considerations are of prime importance for the hermeneutic devotee, but have been given little attention by electrical technicians and information theorists. The term "objectivize" is strange usage for hermeneuts who usually take a highly subjective approach. Nevertheless the actual transmission, whether by voice or by some written or electronic device, requires physical adaptation and moves the entire process into the realm of physics. Voice and body language create waves that are subject to recognized rules of physics. Written language requires obvious physical operations. In short, it may be reasonable to use the term "objectivize" to describe the operation, even though the term may imply more physical attention than desired.

Information theorists seem to have concentrated largely on external noise that may contaminate the message and increase ambiguity. Certainly, these extraneous influences are present and need to be accounted for, but this job is primarily for the technical experts and does not concern us here. Hermeneuts also consider weaknesses in the channels themselves. The channels, for example, may not be rich enough to contain all the desired overtones of the message to be encoded. In some cases, they may be far from adequate and filled with polysematic ambiguity. Thus, noise is present not only in the physical structure of the channels, but also is due to failures in the linguistic structure. These failings are present all along the channels and extend even further. They influence the very structure of the message to be encoded as well as later difficulties of interpretation.

Thus, linguistic analysis is relevant along with electrical and physical technology. Distortions and limitations in the linguistic channels influence the content as well as the structure of the message itself, and they certainly influence the range and richness of the receiver's interpretations. The channels not only limit the richness of the messages, but their fuzzy borders and polysematic labyrinths also must be considered.

It is difficult to assess the relative contributions of the two approaches. Simple external noise fits well into the scientific format and thus can enlist help from empirical methods and modern mathematics. In the tradition of logical positivism, the process consists of two stages. An attempt is made to separate the psychological and more esoteric elements from the more definite physical aspects of transmission. The linguistic approach uses less sharp tools but applies a holistic framework that includes difficulties at all stages. The simplification may or may not be worthwhile.

In summary, hermeneutic emphasis is relatively simple and involves an alien relationship between a sender and a receiver. Two psychological entities are temporally related by the objectivized message that suffers from encoding problems at the start, noise problems along the way, and interpretation problems at the end.

An objectivized message is transmitted through polysematic language channels and emerges in the form of some physical pattern. Interpretation clearly includes much more than simply observing the emerging patterns. Hermeneuts are fond of using the term "understanding" to express not only the act of observing but also the act of translating into consensual meanings. These meanings when combined with the mental environment of the receiver constitute knowledge of varying degrees of creditability. Finally, this knowledge may be neglected or used for decisions and actions. Whether the interpretations of the receiver bear any relationship whatever to some idealized intentions of the sender is problematical, but clearly for communication to be effective in social intercourse some consistencies and probabilistic understandings must be present.

It is clear that the hermeneutical process goes beyond the electromechanical probabilities of Shannon–Weaver. In fact, the entire emphasis has shifted from information theory in the narrow mechanical sense to communication as an interpersonal human activity. Investigation now takes a turn toward psychological theory rather than the statistical problems of encoding, noise, decoding, and the like.

It is tempting to simplify the hermeneutic position by equating channel noise with polysematic linguistics and to separate the psychology involved in sender–receiver interactions. This tendency may be the result of early attempts to make a science of linguistics and to separate its study from the broader study of psychology. This separation has not worked well but seems to have been useful in some scientific investigations where the need is to simplify and particularize rather than to integrate and generalize.

Currently, science is moving in the direction of integrating and generalizing, and the older separation of facts from values is disappearing. This separation at its peak actually penetrated philosophy so that logic was separated from its applications and positivists could talk about separating facts from values, mathematicians could distinguish between analytical and synthetic solutions, and model-makers could separate their models from some external reality.

It is not that this separation – the heart of structuralism – has entirely failed. All sorts of simplifications are necessary for effective inquiry. There is no doubt that the pool of human knowledge and understanding often has progressed by small bits, but synthesis too plays a major part and connections and relationships are essential. In fact, it may be argued that the task of philosophy always has been to further the integration of knowledge. Recently, however, philosophy scholars have reversed the direction and sometimes intrude on the domain of the more particularized sciences. While everything in the mental realm may not be connected by clear-cut concepts, it is clearly a major task of philosophical scholars to help assess shifting boundaries as they change in response to new information.

Specifically, hermeneuts have been concerned with the influence of polysemy (interpretative noise) on the creation of ideas. Thus, they expand the system beyond difficulties in framing the message itself. This expansion and integration considers the influence of language on the process of forming ideas and developing useful concepts. Thus, because of the limitations of language some ideas are never formed and the need for the tasks of message structuring and encoding (objectivizing) never arises.

The idea that the channels available, and the probable noise, influence more than the encoding process has not been developed by information theorists. For a century or so, linguists have emphasized that language actually influences the ideas that are generated. Thus, the modes of language are said to influence the whole process of generating ideas. The ideas that arise are limited and constrained (and perhaps encouraged) by available language possibilities. Thus, the very intuitive process of finding new hypotheses – an area acknowledged to be beyond science becomes closely related to the richness and flexibility of language. At the extreme all thinking is so influenced.

Digression: observation vs understanding

The older scientific literature was filled with references to observables as necessary for scientific inferences and knowledge. Much less attention was given to the broader questions of inference, construction, and relevance of observation "reports" to objectives. Hermeneuts and relatives have performed a useful service by expanding a narrow view of sensual evidence to the concept of understanding. Unfortunately, the latter term itself has too often been associated with semi-supernatural powers and extra-sensory perceptions. An elementary discussion of this development may be of some interest.

It should be noted first that "observation" and "observables" are far too narrow for use in empirical and scientific methods. In spite of attempts to extend these terms to cover sensa from all senses and to include all sorts of technological aids (e.g. imaging devices and microscopes), they often are limited in the minds of laymen to visual phenomena.

Clearly, through tortured reasoning the reports from all senses can be more or less reduced to the usual readings of gauges and measures. These long arguments need not concern us here for the criticism of "observational" science is far more serious. Regardless of the form of reports from the five senses, reports from senses alone are not adequate to support the hermeneutic concept of understanding.

Not only those of hermeneutic persuasion, but all pragmatists, constructionists, gestaltists, structuralists, and existentialists are concerned with the integration of sensory reports to form concepts that are useful for living. It is these constructed concepts related to their environment (specific situations) that constitute understanding. Consider now some practical steps that are necessary to transform observation reports to understandable concepts.

Clearly, to transform observations to concepts requires memory in both simple and complex forms. Memory of similar situations form analogies that are the source of Dewey's "settled" portions of the inquiry. The remembered analogs are then *compared* with current reports (from whatever source) to estimate their relevance (i.e. their "functional fitness"). Among these preserved memories are memories of previous relationships and past structures, and it is these memories that constitute the basis for current hypotheses. In turn, these relationships among remembered situations are judged for their relevance in some *meaningful* way to the current sensory (observational) reports. This judgment constitutes the concept of understanding.

The discussion here has been couched in pragmatic (Deweyian) terms primarily to avoid the common charge that understanding requires some extra-sensory or supernatural power. Whether there are more than five forms of sensing is not important. Whether the reports from whatever senses are available should be subsumed under "science as a theory of observables" is not important. The important assumption to pragmatists is that humans (and perhaps many others) have the inherent ability to structure impressions into useful concepts and organize them to meet the current ends in view. The particulars about what should constitute evidence and what should be allowed to influence judgments and support belief are secondary matters. Visions, inner urgings, hunches, and soul stirrings may have their place in particular situations and for some inquirers; but in science, they seem to be less convincing than shareable evidence that can be subjected to the group requirements of present statistical techniques.

Notes

1 *Editors' Note*: Harvey Hendrickson's notes indicated that Carl considered this to be just half an essay.
2 Claude E. Shannon and Warren Weaver, *The Mathematical Theory of Communication* (Urbana: The University of Illinois Press, 1949, 1964).
3 Yuji Ijiri, *Triple-Entry Bookkeeping and Income Momentum*, Studies in Accounting Research No. 18 (Sarasota: American Accounting Association, 1982).

5 Deconstruction as methodology

For several decades positivists have been severely criticized for their faith in – and dependence on – methodology. Once the consequences of accepting an underlying methodology and its appropriate methods are fully accepted, there is little need for further ethical discussion or other critical discourse. The usual definition suggests that methodology covers the preliminary selection of viewpoint, the objectives to be accomplished, the value system to be used, and the procedures likely to further the inquiry. "Methods" in the same usage means the specific procedures needed to apply the methodology and carry on the investigation. The outcomes from the application of the methods are taken by most positivists to be empirically acceptable without the need for further value analysis and criticism.

In one sense, the outcomes of this process may be said to be "value-free" for the value judgments already have been made before the methodology and implementing methods are selected. Traditionally the natural world has been assumed to be independent of the wishes and methods of the investigator (e.g. the world doesn't care what is done to it and the procedures (methods) do not care who applies them or to what batch of phenomena they are applied). This seeming independence of methods from outcomes has influenced some positivists to believe that their inquiries are value-free and empirically true.

A little reflection shows that these outcomes are not true in any sense unless "true" is defined entirely in terms of methodology. Unfortunately value judgments must enter all along the line for decisions must be made about whether the methods are applied correctly, whether the methods are appropriate for the material and how the outcomes are to be interpreted. The methods themselves may be neutral in some contexts, but their appropriateness is a value judgment and the assessment of results requires human intervention in the form of evaluation.

The assertion that the methodology is independent and value-free is simply preposterous. The objective of selecting a methodology is to accomplish specific goals. At this stage the entire process is value laden with all sorts of preferences that must be reflected in decisions. It may be argued that using market quotations results in value-free outcomes. In the same way, adding two and two or taking the differential of an expression may be said to be value-free. Unfortunately these relatively value-free sets of operations are only a small part of the research operation and are restricted and constrained on both ends by much more obvious value judgments. The tragedy is that many positivists have been convinced that all positive research is value-free. Researchers may rejoice that parts of their research strategy are largely mechanical and require little nonmechanical monitoring, but they should not be carried away into thinking that all aspects of the design are so brainless. In fact some brain effort is required even at the lowest methods level.[1]

Perhaps the most interesting aspect of these proposals is that statistical methods are used not to confirm or disaffirm findings, but to find uniformities – to arrive at hypotheses. (Much of mathematics also is useful in this connection.) In this respect hypotheses go beyond science which is not supposed to worry about how hypotheses are discovered. The artistic part of inquiry often is said to be concerned with the intuitions necessary to sense new regularities and associations. In this area artists (like scientists) need all the help they can get.

These conditions apply to both logic and bookkeeping. Some mental decisions are necessary in logic to see that the specified logical operations are being followed. In a similar way the gods governing bookkeeping may not care to which account is given a debit, but the accountant does care and he must make judgments at every stage of the process.

The scope of science has been circumscribed at least as far back as Popper and the omission of the intuition necessary to generate hypotheses has been standard practice. The remaining duty of science then is to perform an auditing function to determine whether the hypotheses should be accepted or rejected. The interesting point here is whether science by itself has the ability to generate substantive hypotheses. If not, what is left of science? The generation of substantive hypotheses can be consigned to such fields as physics, economics, biology, and the like so that the function of science is reduced to establishing the validity (truth?) of these specialized conjectures. Science thus is a verifying or auditing function without subject matter other than the instructions needed to manipulate the verification or refutation procedures. This function is similar to that fulfilled by symbolic logic and pure (uninterpreted) mathematics. If this view is accepted, the domain of science cannot be free from psychological value judgments and from the necessity to verify the application of the procedures themselves.

Observe that even in this restricted view of science, physical anchoring of propositions and conclusions is not necessary. It may be argued that the tests to establish belief in the conclusions should be left to those who set up the substantive hypotheses, for example, physicists and economists. That is, the tests for confirmation or truth are not a part of science. What then is left of science in this most restricted (pure?) sense? Symbolic logic? Pure mathematics? Strict linguistics? What are the so-called principles of science? And what are its guidelines?

In fact one may argue that science narrowly defined (like pure mathematics) has no principles except conventions for the use of symbols and the requirement that these conventions (laws) be independent of the symbols used. Physicists, economists, etc. then would specify their own tests for validity and truth. Metaphysicists and religious leaders thus are freed from the usual physical anchoring of traditional science and can opt for any tests they feel are appropriate. Science then can become completely formal.

This concept of a pure science is intriguing in itself, but it is not the usual concept. The traditional usage asks the question: Science of what? Thus the usual usage includes some of the decisions and conventions adopted by those who make the substantive hypotheses and support their conclusions. Physicists at one time stipulated physical anchoring of its proofs and the result was a legitimate "physical" science. However, physical anchoring does not serve the social sciences well, and it is ridiculous for an economist or sociologist to argue that his predictions and explanations have a physical basis for confirmation. Some observed bodily presence is not rated above memory, mental operations, expectations, and the like.

This broadening of the definition for science to include restricted methods of observation and verification is not necessarily to be condemned. It does lead to a diffusion of scientific methods and sciences, but this proliferation is not necessarily bad. Yet for structuralists and their associates, the search must be carried on to find the "fundamental" essences of science and thus to establish a generalized concept that lies behind the various sciences and their particulars. Philosophers may feel uncomfortable with the task of finding the essential structure of any diverse set of concepts, but there is a more serious immediate problem: traditionally those who sought to find *the* science often have included some unessential characteristics. For example, there is no reason to assume that the physical anchoring that has served the field of physics well for a century or so is a part of the "fundamental structure" of all sciences. Unfortunately this path has been followed until the general term has been interpreted to require that all sciences have physical anchoring. Unfortunately the requirements of the physical sciences have become defining properties of science generally. Our understanding of the world is the worse for it.

Habermas and deconstruction

Consider now some specifics of the assumptions, grounding bases, and methodology of those using deconstruction as a way of understanding. In the early days of science and positivist philosophy, it was argued that statements may be related to one another in constitutive ways, but at the same time it was asserted that all such statements must establish their validity by being capable of reduction to other statements that can be verified by sensual experiences. Scientists of the nineteenth century constructed all sorts of interlocking propositions that were related in a constitutive way. Some of the propositions made little sense by themselves and could not be demonstrated (proved) except through acceptance of the entire system of which they were a consistent part. Some scientists even asserted that certain constitutive relationships were so abstruse that they could only be expressed in mathematical relations that go beyond the domain of ordinary language. Belief in their validity thus is established by their being essential parts of larger systems which could be verified as a system – usually by sensible experiences.[2]

This requirement for reduction may have been responsible in part for the resurgence of the ancient philosophical cleavage between the correspondence theory of truth and its main competitor, the coherence theory. In the former, propositions are true because they create a predictable expectation about sensory conditions. This view when applied to science constituted the need for reduction and its more specific grounding.

The validity of the coherence position derives from the ancient nominalists. Yet instead of leaving a batch of related constitutive definitions and propositions hanging by their own bootstraps, the intermediate position permits a superstructure composed of networks of constitutive relationships so long as some propositions of the entire system can meet a correspondence test. But correspondence with what?

Related ideas? Some anticipation or expectation? Some actual or possible sensible recognition? Some value structure? Some innate sensibility? Some transcendental experience?[3]

Deconstruction and hermeneutics are based on language and therefore depend on metaphors and the interpretation of analogies. Arrington and Schweiker state: "Accounting is a language; it survives only because humans continue to speak and write in certain ways" (p. 49). On metaphors they state (p. 50):

> [A]ccounting...embraces the utility of metaphors, narratives and vocabularies as [its] raw material...denying metaphor is not only irrational but comes at the cost of forgetting that what is literal under one perspective is metaphoric from another. Metaphor is what makes possible the rationality of the empirical sciences, including the mainstream of accounting research.

The adoption of the metaphoric perspective requires de-emphasis of stipulative definitions and precise logics, and stresses analogs and common language expression. Such a switch in perspective leads to recognition of the need for surrogates, simplifications, proxies, analogies, acknowledgment of polysemy, and for a life lived with hermeneutic interpretations and approximations. Such concepts as income, for example, become linguistic expressions that are related to processes of measurement expectations about well-offness and its surrogates instead of precise definitions with their unique stipulated meanings. The resulting change in approach to conceptual thinking in accounting research can be considerable, and is illustrated by the differences between the newer accountants and their mainstream research.

The most obvious objection to the deconstructionist approach is that its validity depends on consensus and consensus depends on agreement. While this process appeals to those of us with democratic grounding, it may degenerate into simple nose counting with sometimes ridiculous results. There was wide consensus in the witchcraft pogroms, and elite physicists agreed on the characteristics of ether and phlogiston. Before the benefits of democratic government can be used to defend the consensual approach, it must be recognized that democratic traditions require an entire philosophy of processes for determining consensus and the treatment of dissenting beliefs.

It is clear that coherence theories and linguistic programs are bootstrap arrangements with truth criteria suspended on consensual threads that somehow and at sometime must be grounded in common beliefs and values; complete diversity with no common values vitiates any attempt to use consensual approaches to interpersonal truth or validity. Those who hold consensual views adhere to conventional rules to interpret the consensus, and realize that some specific arguments made for certain objectives under specified conditions can be counted as legitimate methods of persuasion. Clearly, empirical comparisons and correspondence with sensory data are among the methods considered to be legitimate for some situations, but they are by no means the only legitimate foundations.

To make a persuasion-discourse system work, certain limitations must be imposed and certain rules for valid argument must be accepted. Many advocates have considered this a necessity and the following quotations from Habermas by way of Arrington and Schweiker are illustrative:

> [P]ersuasion is not sufficient to make a consensus rational (p. 6). (Clearly intimidation, threats and the like are not allowed.)

> [T]he criterion of truth...is not the fact that some consensus has been reached but rather...under conditions which show the consensus to be grounded.[4] (Again consensus alone is not sufficient to support truth. Something else is needed, but precisely what?)

> [A]bsolute freedom of every participant to challenge every claim with every conceivable interpretation of the argument (p. 7). ("Absolute" freedom and "every conceivable interpretation" are difficult conditions indeed.)

Arrington and Schweiker expand the requirements for effective discourse:

> Within a communicative ability *praxis* every citizen has equal status...no domination, strategic behavior or self deception.... Communicative rationality [is] inseparable from radical egalitarianism, a true form of democracy (p. 10).

This conclusion is essentially that of Jeremy Bentham and his concept of equal consideration of individual utilities. Each individual is a free citizen and his amount of utility is to be equally worthy and influential.[5]

A common objection to mainstream accounting research is the implied assumption of a detached observer and an independent world that exists independently of all observers. This view leads to a correspondence grounding that is based on the reports of the five senses. The linguistic (communicative) approach sees the world as a construction of human minds that includes sensa of various kinds as well as such rational attributes as values, dispositions, transcendental experiences, memory, and the like. More generally, the truths of metaphysics, human intercourse, and religion have their own criteria for truth and these criteria may be far broader than "observation reports" so dear to early scientists.

The second broad criticism of communicative rationality and deconstruction is that at the extreme they may degenerate into nihilism and a denial of all values while at the same time asserting the necessity for value judgments at every stage of rational inquiry.

Many have held that abstract ethics and morality are meaningless without an absolute set of values given in a transcendental way. Certainly, not all rationalists hold to this extreme position although most admit its value as a stabilizer in any social order. Dewey, for example, was criticized for his lack of a set of absolute unwavering values long before criticism was leveled at modern deconstructionists. Curiously, Dewey demonstrated his answer in a simple and unswerving way. He argued that at any time the prevailing value system for a social group must be specified or specifiable by the inquirer. Moreover, Dewey himself held certain values with the tenacity of the church fathers. His faith in democracy and the wisdom of free uncoerced citizens was firm and to him faith in – and respect for – human beings and their condition was simply not arguable.

Deconstructionists have their own values and their own rules for acceptable inquiry. These groundings are essentially stipulations that must be accepted through faith. Interestingly enough their values are similar to the values held by pragmatists everywhere, especially Dewey, and the newer approach is an easy transition for older pragmatists.

Unfortunately, a false impression has been generated by claims that deconstructionists criticize by using the values (and presumably methods) expressed in the object texts themselves. I have not found this claim acceptable. For example, scientific criteria are seldom used to criticize (deconstruct) scientific texts. Furthermore, religious texts (especially of fundamentalist persuasion) seem to be rarely discussed in terms of fundamentalist dogma by deconstructionists like Tillich, and similar existentialist-deconstructionists. What then does form the basis for deconstruction? What standards do they apply? Whose value systems are dominant? Precisely how do practitioners apply them?

The charge that deconstructionists have no values of their own is certainly not true, but at the limit such a nihilistic interpretation is sometimes advanced. Clearly such an extreme position is impossible for it is necessary to have some value standards for any judgment. It may be that many decompositions turn out to be negative so that the results are in effect nihilistic, but such outcomes are not the result of having no critical standards. With no standards there can be no judgment and no conclusion.

It may be true as Dostoyevsky had one of the Karamazov brothers state that "If God does not exist, everything is permitted," but many philosophers feel with Dewey that deconstruction can be accomplished by the critical nature of individual intelligence. Actually *any* set of standards may be used for deconstruction of other positions, and there is no requirement for a special standard from God. (Consider Nietzsche, whose "God is dead" message did not interfere with his formation of a formidable philosophy based on the will of certain human beings, e.g. superman (Übermensch)).

As a digression it may be noted that the Berkeley dissidents of the sixties were often called nihilists. Indeed they wished to annihilate all institutional centers of power and destroy many if not most of the entrenched values of the existing culture. In these desires they followed the course followed by most revolutionaries. A little reflection will show that the Berkeley groups (SLATE and related organizations) held their own positive views with uncommon enthusiasm. For them there were few limits on their determination to restructure sexual relations, their advocacy of unlimited individual freedom with its political extension to anarchy and its economic extension to syndicalism, their anti-intellectualism. Finally, their disregard for mature guidance was simply nonnegotiable.

Modern philosophical and accounting deconstructionists (Habermas, Arrington, etc.) also hold firmly to their own systems of values. In most cases, their basic concepts are stated clearly and advocated with great force. Perhaps we can summarize the more important of their bases for judgment.

One necessary value judgment is that discourse and consensus from open discussion is better than closure around any concept including scientific explanations. This assumption has not been proven and may well be unprovable in any general case. The conclusions require some sort of invisible hand to get beyond simple stipulation. Many traditional accountants may still feel that this assumption may result in all talk and little action and prefer grounding of a more substantial kind or from some transcendental source.

The decision to admit members to the discussion club is met by a further assumption. This process is the result of stipulated rules with little proof or evidence (see earlier text) even though there is room for dissent and argument at all points. One view is that being a member of the human species – humanity itself – is adequate for admission to discourse. A further assumption that each human counts equally is a common simplification, but even this egalitarian feature often is supplemented with further admission standards. Some (perhaps most) human beings are in fact excluded or their arguments discounted in various ways. As pointed out by Arrington and Schweiker, humans following "strategic" behaviors are discarded out of hand along with those who intimidate, bully and fail to follow the linguistic canons of polite persuasion. Thus the accepted forms of argument are given high priority with stipulated definitions, and the rigid rules of logic are less important than the looser interpretations of polysematic language symbols and the melding of diverse interpretations. The ordering of relative values is vague indeed and it is not clear whether the sheer number of interpretations is more valuable than alterative criteria.

It is clear, however, that closure and dogmatism are rejected in favor of a process that brings out additional possibilities. Presumably the more alternatives the better, subject of course to restrictions covering frivolity, relevance and delaying tactics. Relevance must be related to objectives, but at least Arrington–Schweiker counsel against closure of a hailstorm of possible expected and unexpected outcomes around a tidy objective function as usually is specified in management science. Some simplification and clustering is necessary to bring discourse within the limits of human understanding, and management scientists cannot be all wrong in trying to apply rules for optimizing and even maximizing as simplifications.

Finally, deconstructionists, hermeneuts, and their relatives are convinced that consensus of "engaged" interpreters is more of a grounding than semantic appeals to objectivity and to reports from sensory organs. This conclusion is made even if the concept of objectivity itself is the result of consensual interpretations. This reliance on communication and language is a development of the well-established view that an inquirer should use his natural advantage of being a human participant and should not abandon this advantage for some ephemeral feeling of detachment and belief in the existence of an objective world in which the observer is not an active participant. The rational communication advocate remembers that the laws of nature are constructed by human beings and that our senses can report only instances of a restricted kind. Ernst Mach believed that these instances were in nature and independent of human interpretation, but some modern philosophers refuse to grant even this concession to a detached-observer theory.

Further comments on deconstructionist methodology

For many decades positivists have been criticized for their faith in (and dependence on) methodology and for their use of the outcomes of an accepted methodology as substitutes for ethical standards. Positivists are not alone in uncritical acceptance of the raw results from applying methodologies. By so doing, they are able to reduce the inventory of their value commitments to the extent that some unfortunate scholars actually believe that no actual value judgments are required in science and many related empirical activities.

Certainly surrogates and simplifications are necessary for all human conceptions, but the answer clearly is not to deny the need for value standards or to select methods without also considering the ethics of their outcomes. The appropriate response is to examine the methods themselves to assess the value status of their outcomes. Once this task has been taken care of, the inquirer already has decided that the ethical consequences are desirable. He selects his methods to reflect his values. Unfortunately, many modern researchers seem to select their methods for other reasons, for example, because they are familiar with the techniques or they are consistent with the currently popular research paradigm.[6]

Consider again the area of consensus. In the Anglo-Saxon tradition the jury verdict, the free market price, and indeed democracy itself are sometimes based on the belief that collective wisdom is more desirable and reliable than individual wisdom.[7] So far as I know, no one has ever tested the hypothesis that collective wisdom generally is more desirable than the wisdom of individuals acting in leadership roles. Clearly such testing is not beyond the limits of intelligent inquiry, and those who assert this proposition might assume leadership in the testing area.

Several reasons can be advanced in support of the position that collective wisdom should be greater. The first results from the possibility that several individuals should be able to come up with better conjectures than one person alone. This feeling is based on the assumption that intuition is spread throughout the population and questions the probability that smart people have a tendency to become leaders. Second, it may well be that the give and take of dialectics and the efforts to persuade will uncover important new considerations. Observe moreover that the ability to persuade is no guarantee that the persuader possesses superior wisdom beyond the personality traits that make him an effective persuader. Power, personality, verbal facility, and the like may be important persuasive factors, but they may bring closure of discussion instead of wise decision making. It just may be that the time and intellectual energy necessary for the politics of persuasion seriously inhibit concentration on the merits.

Third, it is probable that the pool of pertinent knowledge for a group is likely to be greater so that a larger more informed body of knowledge can be brought to bear. More analogous situations should be available so that Dewey's "settled" portions of an inquiry should be more stable. Unfortunately, it is possible that there will be more fumbling around with inappropriate analogies so that Dewey's task of finding "functional fitness" (similar characteristics) between the analogies and the hypothesis may become more time consuming and perhaps more inefficient.

When applying subjective probability numbers, the *process* of decision making usually is held constant and alternative methods are treated as independent inquiries. The result of this indirect approach may be that desirable outcomes result from wisdom accumulated by experimenting with alternative procedures and methods.

Certainly, the choice among methods and processes of selecting analogous situations requires value assignments and comparisons that are complicated. Perhaps, the urge to maximize has been a barrier in spite of its influence in broadening the mathematics appropriate for the case. Urges to maximize actually may be impediments to effective inquiry because simple objective functions may be much less common than a "thunderstorm" (Arrington and Schweiker's interesting term) of objectives at both means and ends levels. Such multiple goals need to be integrated into acceptable mixtures. So far, however, there is no solid persuasive evidence that collective decisions, willy-nilly, will always (or even most of the time) lead to superior understanding and more desirable decisions.

Digression: Lucas' rational expectations and Feltham–Ohlson

The efficient market hypothesis and its outgrowth, the capital asset pricing model, are interesting recent developments that more or less neglected the whole field of accounting and its contributions. Many decades ago, some of us remarked wryly that accountants should seek out the wonderful elixir and incorporate it into our principles of accounting. In any case, more recently there seems to be an admission that accounting concepts and numbers are appropriate components in – and therefore helpful predictors of – the market-value process.

Consider first some aspects of Lucas' re-emphasis on expectations as an important aspect of economic theory.[8]

It is clear that all business decisions must consider probable consequences and that these expected consequences must be evaluated and compared on some value scale. A serious consideration is that before the decision these consequences are *ex ante* expectations that may be held weakly or strongly. These expectations may fluctuate widely and may never be actualized. Along the way new information may be incorporated wisely or badly. Fortunately a competitive social order tends to reward those whose expectations are on the mark and properly evaluated. The converse may also be true so that there is a Lamarckian[9] tendency to entrust important economic decisions to decision-makers who are successful at estimating consequences and evaluating their relative impact. With this potent mechanism for weeding out incompetents and rewarding success, one expects decision making to improve and attain a reasonable level. Since rationality usually is defined in terms of pursuing courses of action that further goals, the public effect is a tendency for society to select rational decision makers.

There are numerous gradations from determinism to complete chaos. Not many intellectuals hold to rigid determinism although apparently hundreds of millions of devout citizens believe in an inexorable fate that directs existence toward unswerving ends. This belief is nonoperational in the sense that it is impossible to establish a set of instructions (operations) within the accepted boundaries of the scientific community to prove or disprove the position. Nonscientific inquirers, however, with wider grounding bases, are able to discard the rigidities of operationalism and construct acceptable explanations to support their beliefs.[10]

The other extreme – simple chaos – is more amenable to traditional scientific rules of proof. Various experiments can be arranged to test whether the individual will of mankind does or does not make a difference in outcomes. The problem from the empirical perspective is to separate the decision areas and determine the pertinence and degrees of freedom in each case. Here again there may not be overwhelming proof that will convince all philosophers and the unrest may still remain.

It is the area between determinism and chaos that affords the most interest. The pragmatic framework here is that there must be outside forces beyond the control of the decision maker. If these forces cannot be modified or responses to them arranged, there is no pragmatic support for making any predictions or indeed for having explanations or expectations. There is of course the possibility of increasing pleasure or decreasing despair simply by anticipating (e.g. consider winners and losers in athletic contests), but this possibility requires an ability to respond to uncertainty in an emotional manner.

It certainly is a commonplace that anticipation may lead to observational or more action-oriented responses and that these responses may change the forces themselves in some anticipated or unanticipated ways. Thus, the very fact of broadcasting expectations may set up the possibility that outcomes may be influenced or even actualized. Certainly, there are limits to the ability of human beings to anticipate so strongly that they actualize the outcomes by mental methods. But clearly with partially controllable forces, such anticipations may influence actual outcomes. This possibility is an old one in physics, philosophy, and economics, but recently it has come to the fore in the Nobel efforts of Lucas. The discussions make hermeneuts and rational communicants feel comfortable and at home.

The situation is magnified for those who make governmental and huge monopolistic-type private policy decisions. A group of interpreters with diverse views requires regulators to assess the attitudes of interpreters and estimate the degree and timing of their responses. The regulators have more remote objectives, and often it is their duty to pursue actions that lead intermediaries over which they have little direct control to alter courses in the direction of public interest. Clearly all excises, taxes, and even laws themselves are designed to alter behavior even though the connections may sometimes be obscure and not well defined.

Presumably, responses in the private sector are made in a competitive environment where each participant is trying to further his own interest. Governmental regulators too need some measures to make comparisons easier. Bureaucrats also need specific goals for their own guidance, and legislators must coordinate these lower level objectives and find some way of assessing their degree of accomplishment. Even if overall goals are dysfunctional, there is a tendency to score regulators and their bureaucrats and to reward them for accomplishment. Thus, there is a strong responsibility for regulators to see that their goals are in the public interest so that rewards and punishments tend to further objectives.

Clearly the better trained and disciplined the regulators, the easier it is to institute further controls and the less the task of the regulators themselves. In the long run, there might well be less need for controls of any kind. So far this condition has not come about and there are indeed more and more controls.

Aspects of game theory become involved when those regulated anticipate regulations not yet announced. In the stock market, anticipations of future movements may lead to present actions, and these actions may influence market prices in the direction of the anticipations. It is only a slight extension to include the probable effects of regulatory actions, but in the latter case the effects may be slightly different. In the stock case the reaction is a probable movement of stock prices toward the anticipated level. For regulators the expected effect is that the need for regulation itself is decreased. To the extent that regulatees anticipate future actions of the relevant regulatory board, the need for regulation itself is reduced, and at the limit a savvy group subject to regulation could follow the desires of regulators without any new rules.

In practice, anticipations are not perfect and worse the nexus between variables is too loose for practical conclusions. The accounting profession owes a heavy debt to Lucas for expanding this elementary concept into a mathematical model with interesting possibilities. Perhaps the concept can be generalized further and used to examine the strength of group cohesion (and discipline) to determine the appropriate amount of regulation in specific areas. The problem is clearly related to consistency in the regulations and to the effectiveness of rewards and punishments in deterring and evoking behavior. Anticipations certainly are easier when there is consistency in regulatory edicts. Unity of the group to be regulated must be an important factor while information and communication also are heavily involved.

The regulators too need to have expectations that are rational and accurate. They must be rational in the sense that they must anticipate the results of their pronouncements and they must be accurate in estimating the timing and magnitude of the responses. Moreover to the extent that their pronouncements are erratic or chaotic, interpretations by those regulated become difficult and this difficulty in turn reacts on the regulators to make their own judgments less precise.

The Feltham–Ohlson model

For three decades or more efficient market and capital-asset-value researchers showed no interest in accounting information as direct influences on the market value of a firm's securities, but it was gradually admitted that accounting might have some effect on trader attitudes and thus indirectly on market prices. In the meantime, accountants tried to understand how important risk-price and related variables worked so that they might be included in the body of accounting principles to improve their relevance.

As a basis for discussion, examine the simplified Feltham–Ohlson model.[11] This model is an attempt to use projected market values for the dependent variables and estimates of what are broadly accounting measures as independent with income substituted for dividends. More sophisticated models adapt the following equation for use in regression programs:

$$P_t = bv_t + \sum_{\tau=1}^{\infty} (1 + r)^{-\tau} E_t[x_{t+\tau} - rbv_{t+\tau-1}]$$

This formulation[12] is only a slight variation from Preinreich and (even earlier) Hotelling, and the variables are defined as follows:

P_t = present value of firm at time t (for this, Bernard uses V_t to denote price at time t);

bv_t = book value on firm's books at t;

τ = time interval for study (infinity for Preinreich, useful life of asset for Hotelling and 4 years that gives an R^2 of 0.68 in the Bernard interpretation of Feltham–Ohlson);

r = discount rate;

$x_{t+\tau}$ = estimate of earnings for $t + \tau$;

$[rbv_{t+\tau-1}]$ = discount rate applied to book value.

The expression in brackets is clearly estimated earnings in excess of the discounted value of the ending book value.

The Ohlson–Feltham formulation brings a fresh perspective to the traditional process. It requires the separation of total expected earnings into unusual earnings by substituting the normal earnings needed to maintain the market value ($rbv_{t+\tau-1}$). In effect the equation requires the estimation of total income over a future interval and subtracts the regular income (defined as the discount rate (r) times beginning book value). Presumably the summation of the discounted excess earnings when added to beginning book value will approximate the net market value at time $t + \tau$.

The first item to notice in this equation is that expected accounting income is substituted for expected dividend throw-off over the interval. The reluctance of modern corporate finance experts to consider accounting income as a useful variable is difficult to understand. Lutz and Lutz, and even Williams[13] a half century or so ago argued that the amount of dividends is not important, because if no dividends are declared the resource base is higher than it otherwise would be, so the investing market is largely indifferent to whether or not the firm makes a dividend distribution. With dividends the stock is worth less but the "investment" value usually is changed very little.

Meanwhile most accountants held to the older ways even though the concept of book value was in general disrespect. Many early accountants seemed to argue that book value is a liquidation concept even though it is obvious that such values may bear little relation to liquidation values. Except for cash and closely related items, it is clear that a going concern assumption is necessary for the service potentials of current assets to be realized at anything near carrying values.

However, even at the time of my earliest essays (1962) many accountants had interpreted book value as a going-concern concept that reflected major service potentials and therefore ought to have some relation to the value of the enterprise. Double-entry bookkeeping often was defined in terms of historical records that show future service potentials and first-order causes of any changes in these potentials. Restrictions usually take the form of liabilities and differences between the total assets, and the value of a firm were attributed to contributions on non-recorded service potentials. Such potentials were disclosed when relevant as goodwill or a similar descriptive term. Ancillary discussions arose about the influence if any of liabilities and whether their presence in an enterprise influenced the value of the residual equity or was arbitraged through the selection of an appropriate discount rate (Paton, Modigliani-Miller, Durand). The entire service potential concept can be traced back to the old capital–revenue controversy that had the auditor examine each expenditure to determine whether it added new potential or merely maintained the value expectations at the former level.

Clearly bv_{ti} (book value) rarely equals mv_{ti} (market value) and a third of a century ago, I was concerned with these differences and the possibility of redundancy. It is unthinkable that early researchers did not investigate the relationship of book values to market values in great detail. One might expect some correlation even though there is no doubt that wide variations exist across industries and even for firms through different business conditions. Room for ingenuity is found in many areas. General market levels – different levels of optimism and pessimism – clearly is a possible factor. Accounting use of historical as opposed to current cost clearly is an influential factor. Mature industries may merit a closer relationship than new, more inventive organizations. Amortization policies clearly are a factor. Tax considerations also may be involved. In the simplest models, the investigator can start with present book value and work through fairly traditional budgeting and other account-related data, and formulate estimates of future firm values. Relevant estimates over considerable stretches of the future usually are contained in budgeting reports and may be used to supplement the independent judgments of others. Research interest here should be directed not only to predictions for individual investments but more generally to firms in general.[14]

The separation of unusual returns is a part of the normal budgeting system, but the "usual" remainder is at best a rough approximation of the Feltham–Ohlson normal discount rate. Moreover, even with clean-surplus reporting, accountants usually attempt to separate unusual gains and losses from more ordinary types so that there is some tradition in both the ex post accounting and the budgeting areas to make an independent separation of abnormal past and expected earnings. The adequacy of the accountants' separation of abnormal returns and the use of the ordinary budgeted return for the discount rate times beginning book value is important as a simplification. The r, as the rate of discount, still enters the valuation equation for discounting the budgeted projections as it has for some number of years. (The four years used by Feltham–Ohlson may or may not be a satisfactory prediction base when the budgeting substitutions are made.)

Since the right-hand expression in the Feltham–Ohlson Model under the simplification becomes the budgeted figures, the discount factor applies only to these budgeted amounts. Some sort of new discount factor that relates the effects of budget numbers to the value added may become a necessity so that the amount to be added to beginning book value will be appropriate. Certainly, just adding budgeted income to beginning book value is not satisfactory. In practice, it may be desirable to work out two discount relations so that differences in the risks inherent in regular as opposed to abnormal earnings may be incorporated.

Some minor accounting matters may be of interest here. It is an elementary observation that there should be little long-run difference between cash flow and income estimates. The income concept as measured by accountants is clearly related to fund flows from operations. Of course, there are minor differences between cash flows and income from period to period. These adjustments are specialized offshoots of statistical methods for handling lags and leads of various kinds in any time-series computation.

In effect the chief difference between fund flows and periodic income calculations is that the latter take an important part of fund flows (that from operations broadly defined) and divides it into a portion that is considered to be a return *of* capital and the remainder which is a return *on* capital. Deterioration of the service potential becomes a deduction from fund inflows and capital expenditures become an addition to the base.

The relationship between book value and total book value also shows up because book value of new assets at the time of purchase usually is taken to be the market value of the asset. This market value in turn may often result from discounting expected benefits so that write-off of the original cost to match with revenues recognized in a period results in applying a valuation process to the original cost so that in static conditions book value should approximate the current value of specific resources. Current cost accounting is an attempt to respond when conditions are no longer stable and service expectations have changed significantly.

To the extent that matching costs with revenues on a service-rendered to service-potential basis reflects some relationship with market value, the chief difference between book value and market value is due to resources that are *not* recognized as assets and to excess expected values that are present in each acquisition, that is, to realized economic con- sumers' surplus applied to the buyer's side. Realized buyers' surpluses are in turn considered to be a part of the contribution of management through shrewd buying policies. Investors who wish to use book values as substitutes (or predictors) for market values must keep this cleavage in mind and devise some understandable conversion coefficient.

Perhaps the strangest feature of Feltham–Ohlson is the use of the same discount rate (r) for both book values and for unusual earnings. The tra- ditional accounting model for goodwill uses a normal rate of return to assets at current values under the assumption that ordinary hack man- agement should be able to sustain this level more or less in perpetuity. Usually, a much larger explicit or implied rate is applied to the above- normal expected return. This assumption assumes that the service poten- tials not requiring asset specification have a shorter expected beneficial life than potentials supported by assets. Often investors have taken an opposing view and have given higher price-earnings numbers to firms that rely more on innovation, effective sales effort, good worker morale, and the like. In view of these conflicting views, perhaps the use of an identical rate by Feltham–Ohlson can be justified.

Notes

1   This position does not deny that mechanical operations may be necessary and useful in selecting a methodology. Thurstone, for example, suggests

that some masses of materials are so amorphous that substantive hypotheses may be impossible. He suggests the possibility of running the usual statistical operations with the hope of uncovering substantive relationships that are not otherwise obvious. The discovery of uniformities is a major part of intellectual activity and is to be recommended, but a sharp distinction between methodological and substantive hypotheses is hardly warranted. The methodological hypothesis may be more diffuse but it too requires purposive planning that requires values. For a technical and penetrating analysis, see Louis Leon Thurstone, *Multiple-Factor Analysis: A Development and Expansion of The Vectors of Mind* (Chicago: The University of Chicago Press, 1947, pp. 55–6). Wesley Mitchell concluded that he had discovered a *new* economics by pouring economic data through the sieve of statistical processes (see Allan G. Gruchy, *Modern Economic Thought: The American Contribution* (New York: Prentice-Hall, Inc., pp. 251, 269)).

2 Operationalists, following P. W. Bridgman, insisted that at least some of the statements must be reduced to definite physical (or mental) operations to determine whether they are acceptable. Young Bertrand Russell admitted only those complex propositions (statements) that could be reduced to simple "atomic" sentences. In fact, it often was argued that the maturity of a science could be gauged by the proportion of its propositions that relate to sensible data. (The opposite may well be the case in modern science.)

3 The discussion that follows leans heavily on the excellent "The Rhetoric of Inquiry and Accounting Research," by C. Edward Arrington and William Schweiker, a working paper dated June 1988. Habermas quotations are from this work and have not been verified. (*Editors' Note*: A copy of this draft has not been found. Ed Arrington could not recall which version of the paper he gave to Carl. A later revision was published here, thus the content of the others could not be verified; the published version is: "The Rhetoric and Rationality of Accounting Research," *Accounting, Organizations and Society* (6), 1992, pp. 511–33.) Page numbers given for all but one of the quotations that follow are to the missing working paper.

4 Arrington and Schweiker, working paper, p. 7; *Accounting, Organizations and Society* (6), 1992, p. 525.

5 For further discussion of Bentham and the utilitarian thesis, see David Braybrooke and Charles E. Lindblom, *A Strategy of Decision* (New York: The Free Press, 1963), pp. 203–23.

6 Braybrooke and Lindblom (1963, pp. 225–44) realize that political systems are too complicated for simple value assessments and advocate the acceptance of many methodological substitutes for explicit value scales. Arthur L. Thomas, an accountant, concluded that his own value standards were not strong enough to override the simple results of letting the period of expenditure be a substitute for the period of matching the expense with revenues. *The Allocation Problem in Financial Accounting Theory*, Studies in Accounting Research No. 3 (Sarasota: American Accounting Association, 1969).

7 The belief in greater group wisdom is by no means the only defense for jury trials and democratic political arrangements. The diffusion of responsibility for decisions may have important educational benefits and

thus indirectly lead to wiser decisions. Certainly, the restrictions on powerful political leaders, judges, landlords, and the like is thought to be desirable. Finally, it often is argued that some decrease in efficiency and even a substantial increase in the number of bad decisions may be a small sacrifice to lessen the greater probability of tyranny.

8 Robert E. Lucas, Jr, recipient of Nobel prize in Economic Science, 1995; see, for example, Robert E. Lucas, Jr. and Thomas J. Sargent, Editors, *Rational Expectations and Econometric Practice* (Minneapolis: The University of Minnesota Press, 1981).

9 Reference is to Jean Baptiste Lamarck, a biologist who is credited with formulating the first comprehensive theory of evolution.

10 Judeo-Christians developed an interesting approach. God knows all – past and future – and has the power to force compliance of all individual actions with His own integrated plan. Even though he knows and has the required power, he permits individuals to have enough freedom to make at least some of their own decisions. Precisely, how the individual has freedom while God already knows the outcomes may interest philosophers but does not seriously disturb believers. After all the Judeo-Christian paradigm permits God many powers that it is the plight of mankind never to understand.

11 *Editors' Note*: What Carl presents here is based largely on one paper, which is an interpretation of two other papers: Victor L. Bernard, "The Feltham–Ohlson Framework: Implications for Empiricists," pp. 733–47; the two papers interpreted by Bernard are: James A. Ohlson, "Earnings, Book Values, and Dividends in Equity Valuation," pp. 661–87; and Gerald A. Feltham and James A. Ohlson, "Valuation and Clean Surplus Accounting for Operating and Financial Activities," pp. 689–731; all three papers are published in *Contemporary Accounting Research*, Spring 1995.

12 Bernard, pp. 736–8.

13 *Editors' Note*: Carl provided no specific references for Lutz and Lutz, and Williams. Carl may be referring to Friedrich Lutz and Vera Lutz, *The Theory of Investment of the Firm* (Princeton: Princeton University Press, 1951) and J. D. Williams, *The Compleat Strategyst* (New York: McGraw-Hill Book Company, 1954).

14 General, nonspecific, levels of optimism and pessimism are presently at work in the exorbitant bonuses now going to even hack CEOs and their associates. Through the years executive bonuses have been an important device for attracting executives to smaller and weaker firms. The idea of sharing the success of an organization with those responsible has a long and favorable history in labor relations and clearly has implications for managerial compensation. The interesting point in recent years is that the stock market itself has been rising at an astounding rate, and executives with stock bonus and option plans are benefiting not only from their own contributions but also from the contributions of exogenous factors. From a social viewpoint such plans should certainly contain adjustment provisions for increases in the general level of stock prices.

6   Comments on academic publications

In more recent times there has been emphasis on what has been quaintly called publish or perish – a highly inaccurate phrase designed to evoke compassion for college teachers who prefer to talk rather than to write. In some ways, this emphasis has led to a travesty on scholarship, but it is my contention that there is a modicum of support for such policies.

One of the sad experiences of my later years in teaching is to observe the struggles of a bevy of young university teachers running around wildly trying to meet the desired quota of publications for promotion and tenure. In the words of a former colleague: "The struggle is to fill a shoe box with every scrap of paper including (especially) high-school themes." One may wonder if such motivation is the proper direction or whether it tends to direct young teachers into directions that are unsuited to their talents. Often, the motivation is in the direction of a quick fix through easy publications submitted before the materials are in a publishable state. In turn, this condition leads to the introduction of a rash of inferior journals to handle the volume of second-rate output. Unfortunately, the phenomenal growth of business faculties eventually meant that the capacity of existing journals simply was not adequate to handle the volume of meritorious research that was forthcoming. As might be expected, arrogance and snobbishness during the selection process was often substituted by the leading journal for the creation of additional capacity to handle the added research.

Some scholars establish their reputations through a modest set of original ideas that require modest publication space. There, folks may make contributions that are so obvious or at least *avant garde* or they may strike a responsive chord with the editors and with the public. Other scholars are in the Schumpeterian mold and make their contributions by integrating widely scattered materials or through historical overviews. The latter contributions require more room for exposition.

Only recently have the journals in our field undertaken more than a wandering *ad hoc* approach to specialization.

It has always been my opinion that publication should come easy for university professors. Teachers who are shouldered with low-level courses should require little classroom preparation and leave ample time for inquiry and general research. Teachers with advanced seminars should be discussing topics at the fringes of knowledge and often have ready-made ideas and topics for further study. The additional time required for preparation of advanced courses should be research oriented so that at best the lack-of-time defense is weak at any level.

In addition, it is near inconceivable that imaginative professors with new ideas would not be eager to share them. Publishing reaches a larger audience than teaching and should be the preferred way to broadcast the word. Unfortunately such is not always the case. Teaching is largely a verbal activity and may be expected to attract neophytes who like to talk, enjoy personal interaction with audiences, and are reasonably adept at influencing others. (Teachers of the case method may be exceptions.) We might expect such teachers to find publishing more difficult and less appealing than addressing professional groups. My own experience among professors, even in some so-called elite institutions, is that glib verbal expositors in business schools far outnumber competent technical scholars. Perhaps this state of affairs is to be expected in professional scholars and the possibility may account in part for my own stubborn resistance to professional schools devoted to accounting. (In some respects, I still am not sure that schools of business are better off when separated from the social sciences or that engineering schools are better off when separated from physics and chemistry departments.)

Looking back with nostalgia may indeed be a sure sign of approaching senility, but in my own early teaching years access to professional journals and the opportunity to publish were exciting possibilities. A thousand or so years ago, publication was a less important requirement for professional advancement so that those who wrote and published did so largely because they enjoyed the effort. Ego fulfillment often followed, although satisfying responses were less personal than face to face interactions. In most cases, responses to publications are delayed. Those who respond feel strongly enough to take the trouble so that there is probably an appearance of more polarization than actually exists. In spite of some opportunities for rejoinders and responses-to-rejoinders, publication does not offer the opportunity to compromise and to work out differences that is found in direct discussion groups. We might conjecture – hypothesize on scanty evidence – that publication appeals to more self-assured less-compromising individuals who depend less on personality to make points and convince opposition. Of course, there are writing (rhetorical) qualities that influence readers and gain acceptance through publication. We are all too familiar with the use of semantic and logical devices to persuade; these include dependence upon authority and historical precedents. Ordinarily, there is less opportunity to convince by the force of personal magnetism in the technical journals.

Certain dysfunctional consequences may result from the need to publish. First, this may encourage a proliferation of second-rate journals to provide outlets for the volume of publications required to man the upper professorial ranks. Second, there may be a relaxation of research activity at tenured ranks to leave available space for younger scholars who need publications for their advancement. We are all familiar with the tendency to publish before the research and the researcher are ready to meet promotional deadlines and to try for double or n-tuple mileage from the same effort. Certainly, some meritorious prospects may be driven from the profession by the difficulties of getting published and the rush required.[1]

Finally, there are the related ego blows that result from repeated rejections and from pompous critics who sometimes help but often leave the researcher with an overwhelming feeling of inadequacy because he did not attempt a different project or design his research to support the critic's ideas. As a rule it is not difficult to be critical of any paper. One simply criticizes the writer for not writing the paper, the reviewer would have liked to have written.

Unfortunately, some editors and reviewers sometimes form buddy paths and take an uneven approach to their work. Each journal has a policy, an area of interest, and a set of criteria for merit. This situation is of course legitimate, but it may degenerate into preferences for insiders who follow or for writers from "inside" institutions. Sometimes, older writers are given preference, and, like colleges that gain publicity by granting honorary degrees, the journals hope to gain some reflected renown from established scholars. Even worse, on occasion one finds buddy preferences based on university attachments, fraternity associations, conformance to some specific dogma, age identification, chauvinistic attitudes, and even racial preference.

Note

1 A Columbia professor whose name I have now forgotten offered advice (*c.* 1940) on how to advance in the academic hierarchy without publishing

at all. The technique was to carve out a vast research project that would be impossible to complete in one lifetime and at each academic deadline to issue a "progress" report designed to create the impression of fantastic effort with results that are still conjectural and do not need to meet the tests of scientific rigor. Such monstrous and receding objectives and tentative findings require little actual research effort and they may generate compassion from otherwise cold-eyed promotion committees.

7 Comments on higher education
The Florida case[1]

The message here is simple: the shortcomings of higher education are due primarily to lack of direction or wrong direction at the policy level. This deficiency is carried down to administrators and through administrators to faculty and students. Unfortunately, this condition has existed for some time, and higher education in Florida is already well behind the level found in comparable states; to achieve progress, a sharp turnaround is necessary at all levels. The intellectual *Zeitgeist*, to paraphrase a former Texas administrator, has been wrong, but in the interests of creating a tourists' dream Florida has already attempted to disassociate itself from the antieducational biases of much of the old South. Unfortunately, despite the northern influences educational interest has remained at a low level. The retirement mentality toward education of second generation children may now be largely over, and the State may indeed be able to continue its recent very modest gains and reach some sort of takeoff level of development.

The first consideration is that of state population and income. Florida in 1990 was fifth in population and sixteenth in per-capita income – a level comparable with Illinois, Michigan, Ohio, and Pennsylvania. It was well above the levels of Indiana, North Carolina, Virginia, Washington and Wisconsin; and far above those of Arizona, Iowa, Minnesota, and Oregon. But Florida's state universities are clearly behind most of those in these states, and there are few high-level private colleges to take up the slack.

Perhaps some misdirection of goals is the result of the rapid growth of Florida. It is true that in 1930 and 1940, Florida was economically on a par with Alabama, Georgia, Kentucky, and Tennessee, with only a slight edge over such laggards as Arkansas, Louisiana, Mississippi, South Carolina, and West Virginia. In those decades, it may have made sense to look to these states for competition and even as models for emulation. Needless to say, the change in economic conditions calls for different role models and for different levels of competition.

Perhaps there is another important reason for comparing education in Florida with other states of the deep South. The political establishment up until about 1920 was made up of essentially southern stock that had the attitudes and goals of the rural South. (The rural pork choppers actually ran the state and its satrapy of higher education until a decade or more after the Second World War.) This tradition, to put it kindly, has been antagonistic to education for a century or so.[2] The rural southern attitude toward education and the intellectual man was often belittling, and sometimes bordered on fear. Far too often, professors were associated with carnival magicians, land speculators, snake-oil salesmen, and bunco artists generally. This anti-intellectual distrust with stereotypes of bumbling incompetents is an important retarding factor in many other parts of the world today.

Europeans often criticize Americans for their adulation of the practical man and the doer as opposed to the more reflective intellectual thinker. Many have wondered how Americans could place Edison above Steinmetz, and some refused to consider any American as an adequate scientist until Charles Sanders Peirce in the late nineteenth century. (Apparently limited consideration was given to Benjamin Franklin with the usual proviso that he did not devote himself wholeheartedly to the field.)

Yet the times had changed Florida and the educational establishment has been painfully slow to respond. The Roosevelt administration with its brain trust and its wholesale help to southern states made wide use of southern politicians at the second level but brought little help to education.[3] (Claude Pepper was in a particularly powerful position to help the educational level in all of Florida but showed little interest.)

Perhaps, the fact that Roosevelt was such a strong political personality reinforced the personality cult that is often the deadly enemy of serious scholars. Moreover, an executive style that hired a "brain trust" may have added to the feeling that the powerful public personality could hire scholars – perhaps not at a-dime-a-dozen as in the Huey Long tradition – but on favorable terms.

It seems that the largest factor for change should have come from the migration of northerners to Florida in the twentieth century. The migration of Jews from the eastern urban centers also should have helped for the Jewish people in general have the highest respect for education. This group demanded responsible newspapers, good literature, and serious artistic performances, but their overall influence on the educational system of Florida does not seem to be as great as one might expect. Perhaps they selected the weaker "sunshine" universities for their less talented, or perhaps these emigres – like migrants from the Midwest – were retired and were more interested in lower taxes than superior educational facilities. Perhaps, they never became an important political factor and could not be expected to exert an important influence. Until approximately 1960, the political structure of the State was dominated by rural North-Florida politicians, and these representatives of the old rural South expressed little respect for genuine education and, in fact, helped squander the invaluable resource of millions of bright young people who might thereby have been precluded from making a much larger contribution. Finally, the fact that there were no heavy private endowments for private schools may reinforce the charge of general disinterest in the intellectual – as opposed to the manipulative – life.

Migration – especially to middle Florida – was largely from the Middle West. Again the typical Middle Westerner was a strong supporter of education. In fact, except for California by far the strongest public universities were established in this area, and Illinois, Michigan, Minnesota, Ohio and Wisconsin ranked with the best private universities. The German–Scandinavian settlers of the West may have been rural farmers, but their respect for education was high indeed. Unfortunately, many were already retired, had no children of school age, and were interested more in low taxes than in education. This group was reinforced by a large influx of retired military after both world wars. These immigrants were handicapped not only by being retired with few school-age children but also by the military tradition of farming out high-level research to leading universities and various so-called "think tanks," and also by seeking second careers for themselves in the political bureaucracy where their highly developed skills of administration were valuable.[4]

In any case Florida's population and wealth have increased rapidly, but statewide attitudes toward education have changed slowly despite widespread breast-beating and lip service to something popularly known as "quality" education.

Turn now to the administrative levels and strategic guidance. The State Board of Trustees (Regents) is primarily a political group. This arrangement is common enough and assumes that the give and take between university administration representing the schools and the legislature representing the electorate takes place primarily at the Board level. Members, unfortunately, are appointed entirely by the political side of the table, and they therefore tend to be politicians rather than educators. Two long-realized dangers tend to arise in this structure. Often folks tend to appoint others who have similar views – politicians tend to appoint other politicians, and if the opportunity arises, scholars might be expected to appoint scholars. Second, politicians are seldom scholars, do not know the difference between scholarship and manipulative jargon and value the former no higher than the latter. The situation in Florida is compounded by the political dominance of rural pork choppers who often took their training at the University of Florida (or perhaps the University of Georgia) which until recently has put an emphasis on pleasant masculine lifestyles and the values of the right connections rather than on excellence in intellectual endeavors. Thus these politicians did not know what a good university should be and often would fail to recognize scholarship in its rigorous forms. It is true that some political leaders have taken their degrees from leading American universities, but their influence does not seem to be dominant. Often these degrees were in professional schools (usually law) that carry their own entrepreneurial what's-in-it-for-me ethic. These politicians know that difficult intellectual effort is required, but they too often associate it with their own profession and not with the necessary work for first-class university work at any level. No one argues that most law schools require high-level intellectual effort, even if they are oriented to small-time courthouse practice.[5]

Perhaps the greatest danger from having strong political boards is that they tend to respond easily to political persuasion. Thus university presidents cannot be successful unless they adopt political roles and maneuvers, and world-famous scholars with reasonable administrative skills but with limited knowledge of political behavior usually are not considered for executive positions. (I too have voted for some second-rate scholars over first-rate ones simply because the latter would be less effective at the maneuvering necessary to get budget appropriations in competition with more knowledgeable and expert deans and area chairmen.) True once in a while a great scholar also has the skills for political operating, but I know of few in the state of Florida. These types must be encouraged even though they usually lose their scholarly fire after long political conflicts and almost invariably are never first rate scholars again. It may be argued of course that such candidates have abandoned their scholarly ambitions before seeking administrative posts, but there may be a number who really feel that they can do more good for the intellectual community by abandoning scholarship and assuming the powers of administration for the scholarly cause.

This view may seem strange in view of my own long-held belief that outstanding scholars are infinitely more rare than capable administrators. I certainly am *not* for ruining outstanding scholars and prospective scholars by turning them into useful administrators. Perhaps aggressive searches might uncover sufficient over-their-prime and disillusioned scholars to fill the ranks. In any case, search committees should consider candidates from outstanding schools instead of graduates from weak schools or academic graveyards. Even mediocre candidates from outstanding schools know what constitutes quality, what has to be done to achieve it, and what is necessary for developing and maintaining a great university.

It is not suggested that all politics and political activity should be eliminated. Presidents are expected to represent the interests of their universities in competition with other universities. Deans should represent their schools, area chairmen and department heads, their more narrow constituencies. Each, in America at least, is supposed to carry the democratic tradition that combines enlightened self-interest, a willingness to compromise, and consideration for the needs of the overall organization including less powerful components and the usual minorities. Questions of group identification are especially interesting at this point. Each executive must identify with all other groups to some degree, and so far as I know no optimum distribution of loyalty among groups has ever been determined. Each president should feel some pleasure in the success of other units in the system as well as in the success of his own departments.

Thus, deans and department heads are necessarily politically oriented. Unfortunately, they often confuse goals. One of their duties is to resolve conflicts and keep their areas functioning. Now it often happens that outstanding scholars are the most difficult to manage. They do (or should) get offers from rival institutions; they receive research grants and apply for time off for research purposes; they often are not skilled in political compromise and often insist on having their own way. Their brilliance has already been recognized by their peers and others and frankly many (like outstanding athletes) are badly spoiled. An unwillingness to compromise may be the very factor that many universities – especially second-rate ones – need. Compromise with existing mediocrity certainly is not what is needed, and a drastic turn around often is the most pressing need.

Unfortunately, therefore, deans and other administrators have an easier time when they hire professors who are team workers and are easy to manipulate. Avoidance of conflict rather than resolution of conflict is less difficult for administrators. Smooth-running departments make life easier for administrators and should increase their tenure. In any case, knowledge is increasing at such a rate that administrators need help to stay abreast of current intellectual tendencies. Thus, tenure limits may be desirable. In far too many cases current appointments are made for unlimited terms, and departments may be consigned to mediocrity for as much as a quarter of a century. Yet automated rotating of department heads and deans does not provide adequate answers. Usually some necessary power is withheld from people who are considered to be temporary, and this device often is a thinly veiled attempt to keep the administrative levels weak and concentrate power at upper levels. Often many who are automatically rotated into such jobs are incompetent administrators and politicians who do not want the job, and resent interference with their research efforts. An interesting suggestion is to limit all administrative terms to approximately ten years. The first five should be sufficient to get the new program under way and the second five should be adequate for effective operation and evaluation. Ten years may or may not be an appropriate term, but life tenure is objectionable and rotating positions from the academic ranks is clearly suspect.

The relative power of administrators and faculties is an important quality factor. It is my observation that the relationship is almost inverse between the intellectual strength of an institution and the power of its administrators. Yet the answer may not be a simple shift of power to existing faculties. In Florida, and perhaps in much of the South, administrators are especially powerful and faculty senates often are little more than conveyers (and reinforcers) of administrative policies to the general faculties. The custom of having the university president act as *ex officio* head of the senate with deans and vice presidents taking aisle seats is simply outrageous. Yet, in these states, the traditional weakness of the faculties means that a sudden shift of power may accomplish little more than administrative confusion. The deans and chairmen may be generally out-of-date, non-scholars, but in at least some cases, decades of intellectual incompetence at the faculty level means that a shift in power would accomplish little. In fact, there is a definite advantage to leaving power in the hands of a few during times of revolution, academic or otherwise. In the typical faculty structure new members (due to tenure requirements) usually come in at the bottom levels with little authority, so that academic changes are likely to be retarded by the traditional views of the senior members. Administrators, on the other hand, often are replaced at the top so that there is more opportunity for rapid changes if in fact the administrators desire to make a turnaround.

A very real problem for Florida universities is the unbelievable prestige afforded to administrators and politicians *vis-a-vis* intellectuals and genuine scholars. One expects newspapers to be biased in favor of the prevailing political powers, but in the South (and in many non-southern cities) respect given to political figures goes far beyond their utility as readily available (and sometimes free) after-dinner speakers. They are the symbols of government (in the general British sense), but more important they often are regular fonts of largesse. As a result, department heads of no ability have more local prestige, more salary, and far more perquisites than their most productive scholars. There is evidence that this attitude is widespread, for many prestige publications (e.g. *Who's Who in America*) list college presidents and even minor public officials automatically as a matter of "courtesy."

The local prestige factor is manageable because in most cases genuine scholars identify more freely with the international community of scholars, and are not concerned with recognition in local newspapers and society columns. (Even recognition through salary increases can be ignored!) Yet many young emigre scholars from leading institutions are astounded to find that their administrative leaders value banal talks to local chambers and service groups more highly than publication of learned monographs. Far too often, speeches and general public relations rate higher than first-rate publications, and traditional (popular) texts rate higher than scholarly contributions. (As examples consider many of the men for whom various university buildings have been named.)

The general result of this assignment of values is that such institutions are widely considered to be academic graveyards and their recruiting pools are limited to other similar schools. The result is, of course, difficulty in hiring personnel who know quality or even care about quality. These newcomers may be very brilliant, for after all some very bright people are always to be found among twenty thousand students, but coming from third-rate institutions they often are not leaders in the fight for change. Really promising graduates often join the exodus that constitutes the draining away of talented scholars and artists from their southern homes. Make no mistake about it, leading universities incessantly beat the bushes within this country and without for talented graduate students for their programs and promising scholars for their faculties. The so-called brain drain is accelerated by students who go to outside universities, discover the respect shown to brilliant scholars, and never return to their roots.

Two dangers in hiring policies may be emphasized. First, the standards for doctoral work vary widely even within the same university. Thus, instructors from weaker schools may be very bright or they may have insufficient ability to obtain entrance in some better programs. This is where SAT and similar tests may be useful. It may be that a minimum SAT of 1,200 plus hard work is sufficient for outstanding scholarship, but certainly 950 plus disciplined slavery is ordinarily inadequate except perhaps for purely artistic pursuits. Extreme care should therefore be exercised when hiring from institutions with low admission standards. Hiring from high-level institutions also offers pitfalls. Even Cal Tech may have a few burned-out students without further ambitions who want to turn off and more or less retire in the teaching profession. Make no mistake, major professors recognize the symptoms and sincerely attempt to match their graduates with congenial schools. It is therefore important for Florida recruiters to emphasize that they want *superior* candidates who are expected to be leaders in *international* scholarship. This requirement short-circuits attempts to match culls with institutions traditionally thought to be inferior. Once a university gets a reputation as being an intellectual nonentity, it becomes difficult to interest faculty advisors or better graduates into their openings. Admission of weakness and dissatisfaction with the present plight is usually not fatal. Prospects from outstanding schools do not expect their new stations to be better so it should be made clear that the hiring institution realizes its need to improve, is interested in improving, and expects the newcomer to help give direction to this improvement. It should be clear that the kind of prospects Florida needs are bright enough to recognize the behavioral activities that lead to success and promotion. Some will adopt the political behaviors but others more stubborn in their defense of scholarship will simply leave, often without a major regret from local administrators. It is important then to monitor the newcomers and reward them for activities that the schools need. Promotions and other methods of positive reinforcement must be changed to express the new direction. Far too often, rewards and promotions have gone as rewards for past service to self-maximizers and even to anti-intellectuals.

The State of Florida clearly has the legal right to select the kinds of institutions it desires. If it wishes trade schools for its universities or an extra four years of high school leading to advanced degrees, there certainly is no serious legal impediment. Yet, if one believes the newspaper reports of state officials and legislators, the state wishes to join the more progressive states in what is known as "quality" education. There is another consideration. Works themselves take on dynamics and the term "university" carries some connotations of intellectual quality and advanced scholarship, and most Floridians probably do not wish to undermine the traditional meaning. Most constituents will probably agree that in this technological age it is *profitable* to develop citizens to their highest reasonable educational levels. Clearly, the social cost of millions of citizens who are seriously undereducated is incalculable.

No one so far as I know objects to trade schools. In fact, the spectacle of semi-illiterates trying to understand Chaucer or Milton in our high schools is appalling. Clearly, such students should be segregated early in the educational process and directed to work that can be mastered. To water down the intellectual content of academic courses so that the feebleminded can be passed is a severe handicap to the educational process and an insult to the better students. There is some objection to calling such trade schools universities or even high schools. Titles should bear some relationship to content and a degree in "electronics" or "computer programming" from the typical community trade school should be distinguished from a degree in electrical engineering from MIT.

The usual response to this objective certainly is not difficult to understand or to implement. We must stop trying to teach Dostoevski and the *Aeorapogedica* to substandard high-school students. There is nothing wrong with this aspect of Plato's (*philosophy*),[6] and of course education must have an elitist touch. By all means establish trade and recreational schools of all kinds, even those featuring areas such as rock and roll, break dancing, standup comedy, football management, plumbing, and pottery making. The point is that these studies need not be confused with serious intellectual activity and be included in the work of universities. Junior colleges are important and most states seem to have done an acceptable job at this level. Four-year colleges that stress professional work (e.g. teaching, business, and agriculture) are needed and important so long as they attempt to improve the operation of their social institutions instead of teaching mature students how to hold their "first job." In many states, the primary need is for high-level intellectual institutions that stress research and fierce intellectual effort and spread respect for intellectual competence and those who possess it among those who so often belittle it.[7]

Turn now to certain aspects of community service, classroom teaching, and research. The Johns Hopkins University oriented new faculty members by stating clearly that compensation was roughly 50 percent for transmission of knowledge (teaching) and 50 percent was for finding new knowledge (research). This weighting may or may not be appropriate for a typical university, but some statement of policy is an elementary requirement. My own preference would be for much more emphasis on research than is now given at universities that are supposed to carry the burden of research. Other universities (in the tradition of the California state universities) may wish to concentrate on teaching in the older sense of classroom performance.

It is true that poorer states may find it more economical to send their outstanding students to other more wealthy states and private schools for specialization and really advanced work. Many states have been doing precisely this with medicine, where medical schools are expensive and the number of students for specialized medical studies are few. For another example, there is no way that universities in poor states can compete with the libraries at leading universities, but fortunately easy duplication and interlibrary cooperation permit specialization at the local level and there is little need to add original copies of Pacioli. The very few students who can profit from specialization in the esoteric is simply too few to justify the expense. Florida, however, is in a different position. With her wealth, it is time that she assumed some of the responsibilities for preserving and furthering the intellectual tradition. This judgment, of course, is a value judgment somewhat different from the cost–benefit decisions that so often govern such decisions. Universities have responsibilities far beyond those of bringing new business to the region.

Consider also the argument that a research scholar is *pari passu* an excellent teacher. Clearly, this is a vast oversimplification. Some students need to be motivated and kept interested, entertained, and encouraged. Others may already be fully or over-motivated and be far too serious to enjoy classroom comedy and entertainment by teachers acting as amateur comedians. Research professors often appeal to research-oriented students and sales types appeal to would-be salesmen. The recommendation here is simple enough: select professors appropriate for the institutions and appropriate for the students at hand. Instructors and students in trade schools often teach and learn best by doing. Where the objective is low-level observation and factual matter, the better teacher is one who can convey these skills with efficiency. Discussing and evaluating ideas is something different, and it is not reasonable to argue that the techniques used should be the same as those used in trade schools. It is precisely the task of first-rate universities to present conceptual structures, ideas, generalizations, abstractions, logical processes, linguistic sequences, and the like so as to encourage and develop qualified students.

Even in general purpose universities that combine many levels, it is not necessary that each teacher be versatile enough to handle all types of teaching. Some degree of specialization in teaching usually is possible in all but the smallest schools.[8] Certainly, it is not necessary that each professor teach all facets of his subject matter, but clearly some knowledge and respect for other views is desirable. Otherwise staff members with stronger personalities will carry the day through more effective persuasion and professional subjects with practical benefits will dominate the curricula.

The question of community service is an especially perplexing one. To justify the tremendous appropriations of state funds some form of direct, visible service seems desirable. What is forgotten is that the chief justification of all schools always is educating the citizens to develop the best available from them. Best in this sense is from the viewpoint of the social group and its goals (e.g. Christian schools emphasize Christian living). Business schools merit state aid because of the increase in efficiency of financial administration and not to find ways to make more money. Certainly, there is little evidence that business education helps amass high fortunes. Agriculture education should increase nutritional welfare for this and future generations and only incidentally should help individual farmers procure the good life. In a similar fashion, medical schools should increase healthy living, legal instruction should help resolve conflicts that are unavoidable in social living, and all should do so efficiently. Humanities are supposed to help mankind appreciate what it has and to add harmony and beauty. Teachers colleges should prepare others for bringing both the competent and the incompetent to avoid dysfunctional activities. Research is not a rarefied element, but instead is designed to help discover new information in all sorts of all lines that will further the goals of responsible groups. Most societies feel that their interests are furthered when all members are brought along and their abilities harnessed.

The overall question of social service is simple enough, it is the implementation that sometimes gives trouble. Some schools try to make their contribution at local levels and accordingly select limited reference groups, such as local businessmen. The political heritage manifests itself in insisting that faculty members be available for free speeches for all sorts of groups. There may be important benefits from this sort of activity, although it must be admitted that some of it is little more than local entertainment that taxpayers expect from their expenditures.

Intercollegiate athletics

One of the most questionable extensions of the entertainment expectation attitude is found in athletic programs at many universities, and a slight digression on university athletics may be of some interest. At one time in the development of the human species, physical prowess was a necessary condition for human survival and it remains so among wild animals and in many primitive tribes. Many groups (especially the Greeks) incorporated physical fitness into their educational systems. Despite some very important negative instances, the feeling that sharp minds somehow ought to be connected with healthy bodies persists and is a part of Western education. This association continues even today in spite of an intuitive feeling that emphasis on physical activity somehow dilutes the necessary concentration for high-level intellectual work.

Just why the physical (macho) aspects of living have survived so long is something of a mystery. Contests with wild animals (e.g. bears, boars, and lions) may have been useful in evaluating early programs, but these activities were usually on an individual basis. Tribal warfare and militaristic man-to-man conflicts may have been expanded to include intramural sports and competitive activities. Thus group sports could accommodate more individuals in each competitive endeavor and maybe have been an extension of tribal survival techniques.

Early American universities were relatively close to the frontier and the connection with survival in contests with animals, Indians, privateers, and border hoodlums seems clear. The rural location of many schools (e.g. Dartmouth) meant that entertainment (except for an occasional brush with neighboring Indians) was scarce and sporting contests served a recreational function. It is only a small step to extend the structure to include other schools. Clearly, considerable interest was added even though the specious superiority established over other schools at this stage of history is on the wrong grounds. In spite of common town-gown conflicts, the townspeople became interested in intercollegiate contests. Visiting personnel and camp followers needed food and perhaps lodging and other services, and local businessmen especially became boosters and began to exert nonacademic pressure.

A question of real significance arises at this point: What exactly is the responsibility that educational institutions have to provide evening and weekend entertainment for nearby citizenry and local businessmen?[9] Whipped up by partisan supporters, intercollegiate sports have become so specialized and so professional that they can no longer be said to provide physical education for the general student body. A former president of Columbia University is reported to have said that professional football has about the same relation to physical education for students as horse racing has to agriculture, and the president of a leading girls' college has wondered about the obligation of his students to provide Saturday night cabaret entertainment for the townspeople.

It is sometimes asserted that the cost of big-time athletics is paid by boosters and related business interests and does not fall on the institutions and their regular financial supporters. In this sense, the boosters are little different from other donors who give scholarships and endow professorships in their favorite fields. To some extent, this is true and there should be no serious difference between giving a scholarship for an outstanding fullback or for a future Bartak. But there are differences. In the former case, the sheer magnitude of a specialized operation can lead to a diversion of power to nonintellectuals and thus, to trivial pursuits. Furthermore, there is a serious question whether universities are an appropriate vehicle for such activity. There may be considerably more wisdom to the path recommended by the students at The University of Missouri-Kansas City that the student body adopt the Kansas City Chiefs, provide cheer leaders, and other loyal activities in return for the right to identify with them in some manner.

At the more academic level the presence of strong win-at-whatever cost departments are simply stupid. There is little need to mention the pressure for lying and other questionable recruiting possibilities along with the pressures on faculties and administrators to help keep marginal athletes eligible. No one denies the difficulty of studying advanced mathematics after running sprint drills and their equivalents for three hours. The more important danger is perhaps the tendency of such programs to make campus heroes of precisely the wrong people for a university system devoted to intellectual effort. Athletics clog the special-case petitions for admission and compete with brilliant late bloomers who can genuinely profit from such exceptions. It is only the exceptional student who can resist the hype and hero worship that so often accompanies those who are gifted with the trivial skills that make stars in college athletics. The most important aspect is perhaps the anti-intellectual, actually antieducational attitudes that often accompanies the aura of these campus heroes. Even their coaches come from the same mold, and in spite of common lip service to educational standards sometimes do all they can to subvert these standards. Some do so only at the margins and on borderline cases – others blatantly and with arrogance.

Turn now to the alleged advantages of dominant athletic programs for the institutions involved. When *The University* wins a crucial football game with a rival *State*, roughly five million fans are deliriously happy and perhaps on equal number are depressed and die a thousand deaths. In years of losses, the wailers become jubilant and the downtrodden become arrogant. Where is the education or intellectual justification for these artificially created crises?

There must be satisfaction for some individuals in order to justify the time and diversion of energy for a winning effort. A number of hypotheses are possible. For example, it may be argued that the misery of losers is less than the joy of winners. The testing of such a conjecture is, of course, nonoperational. Again it may be that the thrill of the contest more than offsets any balance of joy and misery that would otherwise be the case. This conjecture too requires nonoperational interpersonal measurements, and so far scientists have had trouble making such measurements. Perhaps, it is the togetherness and the social event that swings the scales. The question then becomes whether there are other methods of bringing about social solidarity. For example, what about some aspect of intellectual activity?[10]

The argument that a winning football (or other) team is necessary to draw alumni together and increase appropriations is monstrous and may well be specious in the long pull. It should be clear that if only football holds the alumni together in some sort of group identification that includes an advanced educational institution, then the educational process has been badly aborted or at the very least sadly deficient somewhere along the line. That legislators would be seriously influenced in making educational appropriations by the success of athletic teams is monstrous and indicates only that the wrong kinds of people are in charge of appropriations. That individual athletic boosters would think that their contributions to athletics somehow make them a part of the university community of educators and thereby give them privileges to influence educational policy either directly or through legislative channels is even more monstrous if not actually beyond rational belief.

Bodies and budgets

Size in terms of buildings or number of students is often confused with intellectual importance. (Getting a specious superiority over, say MIT, in football may be even worse.) In fact, the reverse may be argued, that is, the effort to increase size leads to lower admission and retention standards. Clearly, huge expenditures for plant and equipment may require retrenchment of research and teaching – the brains-vs-bricks argument of early Johns Hopkins. No one expects classes to meet under oak trees in the dead of winter, and the cloister attitude of many older universities may have encouraged serious scholarly work. At least they may have helped to set the mood. This tradition is well established: towering church steeples for those who aspire to the heavens, ornate courthouses to emphasize the magnificence of the law, granite bank buildings to suggest the stability and safety of the financial system.

Perhaps, the most serious expression of the quantity-leads-to-quality thinking is in tying budget appropriations to the number of students or number of full-time equivalents or to students weighted by some cost-of-education index. No one objects to weighting the relative cost allowances for various types of institutions or for different levels and kinds of instruction. Certainly, the proper teaching of medical students is immensely more expensive than teaching law students or freshmen in the humanities.[11]

The chief objection to tying budget allocations to some modification of student numbers is that the motivation is precisely wrong for those who wish to raise standards, and in American universities raising standards may be the most urgent need. One response is to concentrate on lower-level, easy-to-teach subjects and send the better and high-level students out of state for advanced and graduate study. The resulting loss of brainpower cannot be tolerated in advanced cultures.

Moreover, there is a related disadvantage of reducing attention given to high-level education. Undergraduate instruction may suffer when instructors are selected primarily for meeting classes and transmitting knowledge rather than devoting efforts to research at the frontiers. The instruction itself may become repetitious and deadly and the incentive to keep up with the research of others may be reduced.[12]

Sometimes quality and bodies are related in a strange inversion. A number of faculty members of at least two Florida universities have argued for establishing doctoral programs as devices for recruiting high-level faculty. Some bright faculty prospects may be enticed by the appeal of starting new doctoral programs and thus faculty recruiting may be easier. Of course others may be repelled by the thought of starting with untried students and colleagues. Most would argue, however, that the procedure is partially reversed, that qualified students and faculties should either precede or come along concurrently. The question of bodies is here for in order to justify new programs it often is necessary to demonstrate student demand. Unfortunately, student demand can be manufactured readily by lowering the standards. This effect is compounded, for weak candidates – like poor credit risks – often flock to new programs and institutions after being rejected by established university programs. In short, usually a backlog of substandard applicants is ready and available.[13]

At the operating level there is a genuine threat when admission standards are set low with the hope (or policy) of later raising them in order to bring graduating standards up to par. No matter how hard-hearted a professor may be, it is difficult to encourage a mature student and then after he has completed most of his work to tell him to go home. The psychological wreckage for those who have asked their facilities to make the necessary sacrifices may be devastating. Often such candidates are borderline so that, at the very least, some early warning system should be set up to spot marginal performers. The better procedure is to spot poor performers before admission. The bitterness of rejection is usually less than the bitterness of dismissal after an investment of time and effort.[14]

There is a final comment on budgeting that may be worth mentioning, this is the tendency of administrators to play budget games and present requests well above what is needed and indeed above what is expected. The moral (ethical) effect of such attitudes is degrading and the resulting image of top-level administrators as mischievous boys is ridiculous. Yet this problem can be a genuine one, the line between responsible and irresponsible requests is thin. Some competent would-be administrators simply are not willing to play the necessary game.

Most budget masters would hope for honest requests for what is needed by all institutions and divisions. Unfortunately, what is needed is ambiguous and often open to all sorts of personal opinions and aggressive tendencies. Yet if policy is set in the proper direction, requests may become honest expressions of needs. Overall funds are normally insufficient, and budget authority must have some basis for cutting back programs. The effects of budget gaming are somewhat different. Requests anticipate some level of cutback and include enough hot air to more or less offset these reductions and leave an acceptable remainder. Unfortunately (for them), budget authorities anticipate such moves, appraise them, and seek to neutralize them to arrive at some common language. Resources are lost in planning strategy and more resources are squandered by authorities in discounting claims. The result may be a contest in game theory but the game is not zero-sum, for much effort brings no increase in overall objectives.

Finally, it is necessary for some state officials and university authorities to stop deceiving themselves and confusing the public. Every university, no matter how it is financed, is likely to have a local or regional following among certain segments of the public. This localized importance sometimes infects officials and they too feel their institutions are better than they are. (It is also in their best interests!) Reactions to low ratings are far too often: Who made the ratings? What is their authority to do so? What do they (Yankees, foreigners, eggheads) know about our particular problems? What kinds of criteria can they possibly be using? Even this: each individual school is different and there is no way to compare their merits.

Comparison and evaluation of anything is indeed full of pitfalls and the process is tricky. But it must be done. My own undergraduate college can be ranked as outstanding for mountain scenery and success in soccer, good in religious teaching, poor in research, and exactly zero in graduate study and football. The point is that all educational institutions have something going for them and have some reasons to feel proud. But generally educational institutions are to be judged largely on educational matters and emphasis should be on this aspect. Universities are interested in fundamental research, good transmission of the intellectual heritage, and the creation of an atmosphere that furthers interest and respect for intense mental activity. No problems are solved by trying to escape comparisons. Devising our own statewide tests to use as substitutes for ACT and SAT wastes resources and obscures useful comparisons. Business schools that teach their own economics, statistics, psychology, and mathematics may argue that they are adapting the subject matter to their own peculiar needs. Omit for the moment the very serious question as to whether they need to *adapt* such disciplines, and whether such adaptations are little more than giving a business flavor to the discussions and problems. This sort of adaptation may often be made most successfully in later professional courses that build upon the disciplines. The first danger is that teachers from professional schools often are less competent than those whose primary interest is in their own disciplines.[15]

An intermediate step is sometimes advocated: permit such courses to be manned by the primary disciplines, but keep control of course contents. This arrangement has a built-in tendency to self-destruct, for most professional schools see larger budgets if they can control the courses and therefore the number of student units. Here, as elsewhere, the primary desire to control such courses may go beyond battles for turf and funds, and add to the general confusion. Isolation of such courses often keeps other departments from knowing how weak these derived courses really are. This obscurantist result alone may more than offset the very limited defenses for taking over subject matter from specialists and turning it over to amateurs.

Evaluation, information, SIRS

Turn now to the mutual evaluation of faculty, administration and students, and focus especially on the use of SIRS[16] as a tool for the administrative-faculty leg of the evaluation morass.[17] Any intelligent person working in a university system knows that teachers evaluate students and furthermore, students evaluate professors. Until the last few decades, the latter appraisals were made and circulated informally by the usual grapevine networks. In a similar way, administrators assessed the ability of professors and the development of students. Sometimes these appraisals bordered on the grotesque in all directions, but so far as I know no one questioned the desirability or necessity for such evaluations, and in general such activities were encouraged.[18] Indeed in a pluralistic society these evaluations became a part of the education process itself and provided useful practice for evaluating politicians, employers, friends, family, and the like.

Thus there can be no serious objection to such informal evaluations except perhaps to the occasional nit-picking, personal dislikes, etc., that surface from time to time. Consequently, there should be little objection to more formal procedures for making and reporting such surveys. It certainly is not becoming for an institution dedicated to advancing and disseminating knowledge to object to improved methods of handling information. In fact, it may be that such institutions should further the process by providing statistical and psychological help, for the benefits of such surveys are thought to run to all members of the academic community. Students are obvious beneficiaries of such organized information. Instructors, it is argued, should find out their weaknesses and should work to improve their skills. Administrators were extricated from a well-neigh impossible situation. Since it was no longer fashionable or even seemly for administrators to visit classes, eavesdrop from hallways or pump students, their evaluative cues were poor at best and it is little wonder that they should welcome well-organized information about workers in their classroom activities.

The positive case seems to be so strong and the benefits so obvious that anyone who demurs must be testy to the extreme. Yet there are certain behavioral consequences that deserve serious attention. First and by far the most important probable consequence is that professors, in order to get good ratings and favorable consideration for promotion, will emphasize the required behavior. It is not at all obvious that these attitudes are best for a high-level university that must by its nature deal with an intellectual elite. A similar influence is found in all democratic electorates, where leaders must appeal to the vital middle with its numerous voters. In democratic politics an advantage is that successful leaders (vote getters) cannot win by appealing to the fringes and elites. The result is an orderly succession of power that tends to have the required degree of continuity and to avoid sudden swings along with their rapid vacillations.[19] Not only must leaders conform more closely to the mass of voters but there has been considerable evidence that the type of leader who succeeds in a democratic political arena is not only one with a "popular" personality but he must also be only slightly above the common voter in knowledge and ability. University administrators may be only slightly brighter than their followers. If they are too far above their constituencies, their followers are often not able to follow their arguments and therefore come to mistrust their motives. University administrators may indeed be slightly above the faculty and students in administrative ability, but my experience raises serious doubt about their level of intellectual ability.

It is the use of SIRS reports by administrators to support promotion decisions that is most questionable in a merit-oriented institution. Certainly those entrusted with tenure and promotional responsibilities should use all cost-effective information available to them, and this simple rule seems to be appropriate even when such decisions are made by peer groups rather than by professional administrators.[20]

All are familiar with the dangers of having intellectual institutions fall into the hands of image-makers and become subject to popularity contests of the lowest order. Certainly students like to be entertained, and large sections of the population expect high entertainment from their politicians, from their ministers, and in some cases from our professors.[21] This seemingly innocent desire has taken a more serious turn in educational circles (with or without the aid of SIRS) through the now well-established folklore that it is the teacher's duty to make substantive matters – and indeed the entire school experience – interesting and through this artificially created interest somehow motivate students to serious *intellectual* effort through play acting, comical delivery, interesting stories, and other tricks of the salesman's trade. This controversy has empirical content, although careful study might disclose that such tricks for "creating" interest may turn off the serious intellects that higher education should be trying to attract.

All believe that serious professors should convey the excitement of their intellectual fields and most would also probably admit that some transfer of enthusiasm by crude forms of "selling" may even be desirable. Exactly what is it that we are selling?[22]

Most may agree that a professor can be asked to present his material in more, rather than less, interesting ways, but this recommendation assumes that it is desirable to have competitive market activity among the various lines of intellectual pursuit – a debatable question. In any case it does not follow that the usual forms of "making the class interesting" for run-of-the-mill 20-year olds will develop sustained interest in the areas of intellectual activity and cognitive inquiry that universities are trying to foster?[23]

Clearly there are differences among teachers and such differences can be expected to appear in classrooms and to appeal with varying force to a diverse student body. Some students may be self-motivated intellectuals regardless of the subject matter and need no explicit (certainly no contrived) efforts in this direction. Others may be caught up in the excitement of the subject matter itself, that is, astronomy, physics, and art. Others may be helped by watching a skilled professor approach intellectual activities. A few may become interested in algebraic geometry by the entertaining antics of an instructor, but somehow the connection between serious mathematical study and party noise makers seems vague and obscure. Why is there so little attention to information about the range of a field, its opportunities, special intellectual requirements, interesting interdisciplinary facets, and required life styles? Perhaps it is hair splitting, but the absurdity of a distinguished professor's applying Dale Carnegie's selling techniques or Norman Vincent Peale's simplistic optimism to, say, Coptic philology should at least be mentioned.

Another argument for restraint in the use of student surveys should be mentioned: student knowledge of what is required and therefore what constitutes good teaching is likely to be biased. How is a beginning student to know what material is to be mastered in the introductory course in calculus? How is he to know what subjects should be emphasized, what items should be included in tests, and the required competence necessary for future work in engineering, physics, or mathematics? Yet there is a more telling criticism of his judgment, for he is always judging the present course by his earlier, lower-level courses. Students just out of the lower division, where emphasis often is on presenting facts and building specialized vocabularies, tend to judge more advanced courses in terms of their interest and success in elementary or more general courses. Thus, the students' judgments are likely to be from a lower-level base – lower division by high-school standards, upper-division by lower-division standards, and graduate courses by undergraduate norms. To complicate matters introductory courses often are more general in order to provide students an introduction to the entire field (e.g. economics, physics, psychology), so that many students feel that a superficial survey is all that is required and therefore resent the more careful, less broad, and in-depth blasting that is the hallmark of more advanced work.

In a similar way, students from undergraduate courses judge graduate courses primarily on the basis of what worked for them as undergraduates. As a result, they sometimes resent the Socratic interchange and other (often laborious) attempts to develop their own intuitions to sense the original relationships that are necessary for productive thinking. Such courses put less premium on teaching facts and standardized models, and more on the tedious development of independent intellectual skills. Criticism, judgment, and value orientations suddenly become more important. In fact, it may be argued with some justification that the quality of some graduate courses is inverse to the amount of new factual material and standardized models introduced.

How can the student be aware of these changes in teaching objectives and evaluate them when his knowledge is invariably from lower, less demanding levels? At the end of the term he may indeed feel cheated when he attempts to outline what he has learned, for almost invariably a greater pool of facts are learned in introductory courses and through lecture methods. Perhaps, instructors can improve the situation by explaining their objectives in clear terms at the beginning of the course and continuing to stress them throughout the term. Yet even this useful process is not likely to satisfy the ordinary student who has not done so well in the course after being successful at lower levels with their techniques of learning, summarizing, and repeating.[24]

Some other behavioral effects of using SIRS for faculty appraisal may at least be mentioned. For example, there may be a tendency for teachers to give higher grades, for students may be disposed to give higher assessments after receiving ego-satisfying marks. Perhaps the professor may cover less material, cover existing materials less thoroughly, or demand less of students, and thus create a more comfortable classroom environment. Tests and examinations may become less stressful, and classroom time may be taken from serious intellectual study and devoted to entertaining anecdotes and experience. More disruptive student behavior may be condoned.

Turn again to an administrative use of student evaluations as an important determinant for promotion. Perhaps the most important consequence for professors in critical areas is the resulting feeling of being watched – of being spied on – a familiar feeling for natives of totalitarian countries and an altogether unacceptable situation for professors who need some academic freedom for dealing with sensitive material. (Even workers resent time-and-motion studies with stop watches hiding behind factory posts.) Everyone should know that they are continuously being evaluated in all sorts of activities necessary for living, but certain techniques often are regarded as highly questionable, for example, classroom visitations by administrators, course-outline approval by various gate-keepers, censured book lists, and required responses to long lists of specific questions that often are not relevant to a teacher's main activities.

In fact, it may be argued that in high-level universities and research institutes, administrators should have *no* power of promotion or retention or even veto power over people whose work they often do not and cannot understand. Clearly some administrators, especially those in good intellectual institutions, may have sufficient knowledge in one or more fields, but it is highly unlikely that they are capable of judging quality in many academic disciplines. (Even professors within a fairly narrow field, e.g., mathematics, often are unable to understand the research of their close colleagues.) Furthermore, most (not all) university administrators were never serious scholars in any academic field and thus were never capable of judging serious quality. The situation is improved somewhat when recommendations for additions and retentions come from specialized colleagues who do know quality in the area. But even here there seems to be no reason to allow administrators to have gate-keeper (veto) powers or any other kind of authority except perhaps some loose budgetary controls. And these restraints should be weak indeed.

What about the use of SIRS reports by faculty committees to evaluate members of their own groups. Usefulness here is mostly confined to confirmation of information from other sources. Teachers who are actively engaged in teaching certainly should be able to make reasonable guesses about the teaching ability of colleagues. After all it is their own life's work. Furthermore, professors should already be aware of the balance or unbalance of the types of techniques and abilities possessed by those in their departments. In most cases, there is a tendency of staff members to gravitate to the levels of teaching they do best. Furthermore, colleagues already have considerable interaction with students, and students being natural bitchers unless specifically discouraged often will gossip about teachers. In general, SIRS is a more formal and more desirable way of collecting these attitudes and are thus to be preferred over informal gossip paths.

While we have concluded that SIRS are of limited help to faculty members and administrators, it remains to discuss the therapeutic effects on the students themselves. Students who genuinely dislike an instructor may use the SIRS forms as an opportunity to retaliate for all sorts of real and imagined grievances. In a similar way, students with tendencies for hero worship may welcome the opportunity to set forth their inner feelings. Yet these reports tend to reflect student feelings at the time. What about students who change their minds ten years after college and realize that a professor hated at the time now appears to have been one of their very best? This feeling is of course a common result of having to make immature judgments without adequate background, and is common to all decision-makers. It may be argued that so long as students are not homogeneous in their objectives and preferences, the faculty too should not be homogeneous. In fact, many universities recognize this possibility and try to have at least one professor whose style will be congenial for any type of worthy student. One may appeal to intuitive dreamers, another to hard-headed pragmatists, still another to those who need much personalized attention, and (rarely) one who is completely uninterested in students as individuals and concentrates entirely on intellectual matters.[25] Some students, for example, are enthusiastic about an accounting teacher who uses classroom time to go over each transaction and every facet of homework assignments. Those of us who already have done the homework were almost invariably bored with this type of teacher and took special effort to sit near the windows or close to unmonitored exits.[26]

Comments on no-value education and discussion

In this section, we hope to consider some aspects of neutrality in teaching in schools and universities. The question of value-free education and its alternatives is especially important in pluralistic societies, where differing viewpoints are contending endlessly for political and moral supremacy.[27]

Ask first in a simple context how in an open society is a university education to be divided among subjects such as business, humanities, and physical sciences? Even simpler: How many hours of accounting should constitute a major? How are these decisions made? In what sense can a decision maker be neutral? Precisely how does he make a decision without values? For later discussion: How does a school system communicate moral, ethical, and political values to its students? Consciously? By indirection? By default?

The concept of neutrality is not the easiest to dispatch for it is clearly impossible to be neutral to all parties that might be concerned. The student may not be coerced in his selection of psychology over economics, but the very fact that these courses are offered and that he is required to select speaks for the existence of educational values. Absence of sociology, anthropology, or philosophy from the elective panel conveys a feeling of lesser importance. The very fact that schools exist – even with no requirements whatever – broadcast the desirability of education in some form. Neutrality in the selection of subject matter, studying or not studying, attending or not attending, financing or not financing results in a bizarre educational system.

The fact that resources are devoted to the study of accounting suggests that accounting services are thought to be worthy, and the same may be said for other branches of business and indeed for all learning. Since neutrality is difficult or impossible, whose values prevail in an American school of business or university? The institution is a pluralistic structure and somehow these decisions must be made and explicitly or implicitly somebody must make them.

Since these decisions must be made in some fashion, one may ask how they are likely to be made when the top policy makers aim at neutrality. It is not enough to make a sharp distinction between policy and administration or to blame fuzzy guidelines from whatever source, for obviously certain values must always be settled somewhere in the system.

In any society all participants – professors from all fields, administrators, voters, students, religious leaders, and even zealous legislators bring some values and some limited power to implement them to the process. In some instances, a single power center may be strong enough to impose its will on the others. But even in such totalitarian systems pockets of influence and power remain throughout the system. A teacher may shift emphasis within a course, some teachers may spend most of their free time reading religious tracts instead of sports manuals. Moreover, it is impossible for even a dictator to turn aside all direct advice from his friends, cronies, and advisors. Influence is exerted in all sorts of ways and at all sorts of levels.

The present educational process is a modified balance-of-power structure. Broad functions are set forth and related roles are loosely defined. Some recommendations along with some broad prohibitions are set forth and the participants are turned loose to fight it out by exercising the roles assigned to them. The results are loosely monitored by the electorate (or its representatives) and on occasion steps are taken to modify the course. Deans battle deans. Department heads vie with opposing heads. Professors grapple with professors. Faculty wives snarl at faculty wives. Students often seek to expand their role. Conspiratorial parties and political nice guys rush to support their views. Wealthy alumni endow specialized chairs in their fields of interest; many more become "boosters" and attempt to tip the scales toward gladiator sports. In some sense, the vectors of power may indeed be countervailing so that some sort of equilibrium or steady-state conditions may result.

In America, the value question reached red-hot levels in connection with religion and with communism and related ideologies that state without pretense that they wish to destroy the present state, and in the process alter the value structure that the school system encourages. More recently, the emphasis has shifted to ethnic diversity and away from the predominant values of the male Anglo-Saxon establishment that emerged from past power struggles.

Traditionally, the question has been hottest in the church–state controversy. The struggle has carried through with scarcely diminished intensity from the days of the early settlers. Most students are educated in public schools and the American electorate has consistently resisted the merging of church and state even though much of our political pageantry is based on religious rituals, our values are largely Judeo-Christian, and the official state position is tolerance to all religious beliefs. Biblical values could be and were taught without restraint in church-related institutions and the usual procedure was to teach religious values in public schools without involving churches and church politics.

An interesting extension came with the teaching of general ethical values that were only indirectly upper directed or religiously sanctioned, for example, hard work, fair play, non-adulterous sex, mental and physical dissipation. In the early days, these supplementary values were also sanctioned or reinforced in schools and such popular textbooks as *McGuffey Readers* were designed to extend and expand Aesop's fables into the nineteenth century. Aesop's fables combined the teaching of the values advocated by those in power with amusing stories that appealed to the young – a sort of *Sesame Street* but with values perhaps more boldly and specifically delineated. It is quite possible that a large minority or even majority of the Hogarthian characters of that time did not concur and may have resented paying tribute in the form of taxes to support values that were so foreign to their own. The *McGuffey Readers* and other school materials of the second half of the nineteenth century were even more directly related to values in education. So far as I know, these texts were not aggressively religious in their orientations, but they certainly emphasized the values advocated by protestant Christian groups.

The fairly recent rejection of religious observances such as prayer in public schools is an interesting development. The present political power centers apparently weighed the consequences and decided that the possibility of reuniting church and state was more dangerous than the affirmation of values and observances that were essentially Christian in public schools. An extension of much more gravity followed the prohibition of teaching explicit Christian values in public schools. This prohibition was at least rational in terms of the shifting values that resulted from the new balance – the new consensus. The really serious extension came with the fostering of the *impossible* objective of refusing to teach *any* values in such schools. In America it is somewhat difficult to reconcile the refusal to teach the professed values of its own social structure with the long-continued attempt to make the country a melting pot, create homogeneity and decrease the tendency toward pluralism that inevitably arises when so many people from different backgrounds are brought together. The fear of a unification of church and state may still be great, but why this fear should carry over to opposition to the teaching of all values is not so clear.

It seems that other arguments are usually advanced to thwart the teaching of values. First, it is sometimes argued that it is not "fair" to prefer one set of values over another in public school systems. This argument – as with most "fairness" arguments is specious. There is no a priori reason why a social group should not try to preserve its values by propagating them and transmitting them to its youth. So long as freedom of religious belief and ethnic customs is the guiding principle, it is essential that those with differing views should be free to practice them. Yet whether freely held competing values need "equal time" in the school system is an entirely different question and one that many can honestly answer in the negative. The values held by a society naturally are nearer to some alternative beliefs than others. The question is whether the teaching of those values are therefore undesirable (unfair?). Many feel that it is the free opportunity to observe and to teach privately that matters most, and the negative argument that minority holders of values are taxpayers and therefore contribute to the public school system is not convincing. Members of society – and all are paying members – at some time in some way are forced to contribute to groups, individuals, and causes with which they disagree. The very nature of taxation, legal damages, etc., are interpersonal allotments of this sort. Indeed the opposite view is also arguable – there is always a genuine cost (sacrifice) to the majority of supporting a pluralistic society.

The most ridiculous argument of all is that the school system of a social group should not teach values because its values may be (or could be) wrong when judged by different standards. This argument is infantile. Since when is anyone sure he is right on any matter of fact or value? People who are sure have often proved to be the most dangerous to human association. When opposing value systems can be freely taught somewhere in the system, an avenue for change is available. Preserving such an avenue is of great importance and helping to provide a theater for displaying opposing views is clearly desirable, but for the majority to be unable to advocate its own values is strange doctrine indeed. It may be argued with some validity that the majority has no right to insist that minority members help foot the bill, but in a mixed open society this argument is difficult to implement. All are familiar with allocation of resources to roads, police forces, hospitals for the aged, etc., and in all such cases costs and benefits are shared unequally by all individuals and groups. The limit to this argument is that anyone should object to contributing to any society whose views differ from his own. There is no position that does not seem unfair to some members. It is for this reason that fairness as a general guideline is difficult to apply to educational work and to accounting as well. For a lazy man to be taxed to support those who teach the protestant ethnic of thrift and hard work is not likely to be popular with members of the lazy group. (An opposing argument may be advanced: the lazy man may wish for others to support the work ethic and argue hardest for compassion.) Alcoholics may oppose taxes to support bans on spirits, and whore-mongers may believe that his forced contributions for prohibition of public whorehouses is monstrous.

Turn now to recent discussions of whether communists, fascists, KKK, weathermen, Hell's Angels, general blackguards, psychotic murderers, etc., should be allowed to advocate their values and especially whether the school system has an obligation to see that students hear their stories. In one sense this situation may be restated into the question of to what extent, if any, an open society is obligated to see that those endeavoring to tear it down have equal (or adequate) time to do so within the public educational framework. The question as to whether they should be permitted to do so within their own private educational organizations is another matter. There is a common core on the responsibility of a regime to try to perpetuate itself. In general terms, there is a trade-off of values: the exchange of some values of a democratic regime for some increase in freedom of speech.

This argument often reduces to the alternative of having values presented by ardent advocates or of having them presented as "objectively" as feasibly can be done. My own attitude encourages the hiring of such antiestablishment people with the provision that they use only those persuasive methods acceptable for intellectual activity generally. This latter restriction is due to my own deep commitment to free inquiry (without harassment) and the duty of scholars to represent their findings, conclusions, opinions as faithfully as they can and be willing to discuss opposing points of view. This concept (like all such ideas) is clearly fuzzy at the edges, for it brings up such vague concepts as truth, accuracy, faithfulness without which we cannot function. The duty of the state to protect itself and its institutions is less certain in my mind. There is always the problem of which group to identify with, and in recent discussions the accepted top value is that of "mankind," "humanity," etc. It happens that my own values rate democratic social institutions *very* highly (but not necessarily as supreme) and therefore I would trade them off only in extreme instances. Yet the freedom of dissent and to persuade by certain methods is a part of the democratic tradition, and it too must be given up only on extreme terms. Such tradeoffs occur in most ethical or moral situations, for if there were no conflicting values, there would be no need for ethics or morals. My willingness to permit the emotionally disturbed as well as more acknowledged rational people to scream that our president is a "capitalist, imperialist murderer" even if he does not deserve it and the screamers do not actually believe it may need further explanation.

My willingness to let crazies present their cases even though my belief is that their statements are distorted or untrue is not related to the oft-used argument that it is impossible to get balanced, unbiased, or neutral expositions. Everyone is biased from some points of view, everyone is unbalanced from a different set of perspectives and anyone's neutrality may be questioned. Rather my argument proceeds from a feeling for consistency with our usual democratic procedure of advocacy. Our courts hope to separate the wheat from the chaff even when each litigant, following his own interest, presents his "facts" and his conception of the issues of law in his own biased way. Good democrats feel that the electorate can reach tentatively acceptable discussions in the midst of political bombast – a bombast that frightens some outsiders. My own opinion hinges precisely on this point.

In order to perform the judging function effectively in politics, judicial matters, or purchasing some sort of training or experience may prove to be necessary. Certainly teachers are not doing students a favor by shielding them from opposing views, and protecting them from anti-establishment arguments. It is precisely this kind of experience with bombast that is needed by all educated people who must render judgments and reach conclusions.

A related question arises regarding the importance of maturity. Various stages of maturity may be identified, but the setting of an age or date for rationality is too simplistic and is question begging. Usually universities try to encourage rationality and consideration of the consequences of actions chosen. At one extreme, some scholars have succumbed to the total absurdity of human existence and to the hopeless feeling that there is no useful concept of rationality. Various churches have emphasized the need to "get them young," and clearly some attention needs to be directed to the fixing of belief and the development of value sets. A few have argued that faith and the fixing of belief are not rational and that rationality is not necessary and may not even be desirable in a democracy or good society.

My own sentiments are on the side of rationality – at least partial rationality – and I believe that students need to become accustomed to bombast of all kinds and intensities. This belief means a negative reaction to the using of balanced discussions and its related concepts. Students may become so accustomed to balanced discussions that they fail to analyze ridiculous statements and develop the habit of being uncritical and making their decisions only in a "reasonable" environment. If so, they can become confused when confronted with extreme positions with shrill and strident support.

Anti rationalism

Decades of reflection have left me still with unresolved doubt about the benefits of old-fashioned logical argumentation. Yet, I am not persuaded that human beings are relentlessly antirational. The usual definition – that man is irrational when he *knowingly* makes decisions or takes actions whose consequences thwart his value system – is acceptable so far as it goes and certainly is superior to a definition that compares a particular value system with other value systems, even if they are proscribed by inner or upper sources, peer-group pressures, or broad social usage.

The first definition of irrational in terms of consistency of decisions with values has been a useful definition in an indirect way. If a person's decisions do not further his objectives, he may simply lack knowledge and is doing the best he can with imperfect information. No one, so far as I know, considers this kind of failure to be irrational, even when the decision-maker may have been able to further his objectives by searching for better information or by discontinuing the search and acting sooner. There is of course no way of looking into a man's subjective orientations and clinically observing patches of irrationality. Yet the definition is not tautological because there are research techniques for drawing inferences about values, for disclosing inconsistencies, and deciding whether the inferences are essentially correct. (We neglect here the possibility that inconsistency itself is an objective.)

My own uneasiness is concerned more with argumentation itself in an increasingly sophisticated society. This unease has a long history, but has become more demanding with the events of the last few decades. The beginning student of philosophy cannot help admiring some aspects of Sophist doctrine and recognizing that any position may be supported or refuted by nominalist arguments.

The Judeo-Christian arguments, as I understand them, tend to enlarge, recycle, embroider, and piece together a mosaic of impressionistic analogues and related images. The result is not exactly antirational (antilogical), for there are many implied antecedent–consequent relations and assumed value systems. The Zen movement, now currently popular in the Western World, is based largely on the utter futility of argumentation. The gentle guru, like the equally gentle Jesus, may sometimes display impatience with those who do not understand, but the fact is that their values and their messages may be difficult to reformulate in Hellenic logical forms.

Teachers of rhetoric, lawyers, and debate coaches have long been aware of the possibility of arguing *any* facet of *any* proposition. All are familiar with the conditioning devices used by debate coaches, for example, "Talk for five minutes on unicorns," "Argue that motherhood should be outlawed," and equally ridiculous topics. Judicial officials have become adept at sensing the shared values of their constituencies and rejecting arguments that are inconsistent with them.

The recent existentialist movement has also stressed the futility of logical argument. To some extent, this attitude is an extension of the futility found in the human condition. The literature and theater of the absurd of the mid-century is an interesting extension. That goes far beyond the absurdity of logical explanation.[28]

The recent student uprisings at Berkeley and elsewhere – unfortunately with some of my former students enthusiastically carrying banners – are examples of an essentially anti-logical, anti-explanatory, anti-principle approach. Clearly any position may be supported by arguments, and without shared values (including logical inquiry) one argument may seem to be as good as another, that is, "My ethics is as good as your ethics."

Perhaps the best an intellectual can do is to attempt to find the values that support various stated positions. But even this pleasure is not allowed, for such inference rests on logical procedures, and activists are not bound by such rules. Four-letter words screamed at sheltered spinsters or at members of ethnic groups may be condemned or condoned, depending on the values employed. The innocent bystander shot by mistake "should not have been where he was." The parents of a murdered child are responsible because they did not furnish ransom. Possible illustrations are without end. Racial epithets are *bad*; four-letter words are *good*. There are no bad people – just *bad* switch blades and hand guns.

For a social order that is not splintered beyond recognition, a set of values sooner or later does emerge. Changes are congenial to some and anathema to others. The ethics of those of us past 30 may indeed need serious modification and the same may be said for the ethical ideas of those less than 20.

Where to stand in these changing winds of doctrine? For my part, the guiding rule has been relatively simple although it may be far from universally accepted. I am a stubborn believer that inquiry should be free from coercion in all universities. Thus my guideline, for a myriad of recent problems in universities is simple: if an action tends to further free intellectual inquiry, I support it vigorously. If not, I am firmly against it. But is there a higher value for which such freedom might be sacrificed?

I wish to express my own views in an unmistakable manner. An intellectual – and a university of intellectuals – must listen to any and all viewpoints, and must be able to express varying viewpoints. Faculty members must not be intimidated and certain topics must not be placed off limits. It is a saddened heart that finds audiences at first-rate universities screaming like frenzied street mobs in order to keep a viewpoint from being expressed. "Free speech" must mean *free* speech. Yet value systems – implicit or explicit – at free institutions are clearly worth saving. The practical problem is how to mobilize the powers of inquiry and the intellect to combat groups set on destroying them. One of my closest friends believes the intellectual establishment and democracy generally are fragile institutions and feels that if they cannot survive by their own rules, they should be permitted to die. I cannot accept this view. Some things are more important than others and all decisions require that some lesser values be traded off. The irony is in the paradox of having to give up at least temporarily your own supreme values in order to preserve them. Yet a democracy and a university are not required to be pacifistic. Good democrats can fight for the essentials that are necessary for the proper functioning of democracy. But is unlimited free inquiry more important than preserving the institutions that support it?

Notes

1 This piece is written from a sympathetic Southern perspective but unfortunately it applies to many non-southern universities as well. Since these notes were written some Southern universities have made remarkable progress. Others like Johns Hopkins never did merit such critical appraisal. Occasional mention of Florida and Louisiana public universities is due to my first-hand experience and not to any attempt to denigrate their sincere efforts to improve.

2 W. J. Cash, a sympathetic native southerner, has discussed this problem and the century-old brain drain from the South in considerable detail. His argument is that the vacillating cotton markets and financial panics of the early nineteenth century led to bankruptcies and takeovers so that the plantations and with them the political power no longer belonged to the former aristocrats. The new bourgeois owners tried to keep up appearances of the former owners but tended to convert their libraries from Burke, Berkeley, and Plato to the equivalent of Dale Carnegie or his simplistic antecedents. Apparently, the anti-intellectual (especially fear of education) attitudes carried over to refusal to educate slaves, to the poor whites and through them to the aggressive self-maximizers who wrested control of the rural wealth and the culture during adverse times. Cash adopts the somewhat limited view of a rural or small-town piedmont southerner, and is on the whole sympathetic toward southern attitudes and values. W. J. Cash, *The Mind of the South* (New York: Alfred A. Knopf, Inc., 1941). Passim.

3 This is not to deny that the US Department of Agriculture helped land-grant colleges. At one such school by far the best statisticians on the campus were those in agriculture, in other cases the agricultural economists were clearly more modern than members of the economics department. My own introduction to industrial engineering came from an astute agricultural engineer financed through this agency.

4 In general through the years I have been opposed to business schools hiring retired military personnel as professors. These people are highly skilled in surviving and being effective in bureaucracies, and often make bumbling professors seem more ineffective. The result is that the military types often develop more power than is warranted by their knowledge of the educational process. Often they become high-level administrators in relatively specialized areas without an interest in intellectual activities. Often too they have a tendency to place these activities on a lower level than the ability to survive and manipulate various individuals and groups. Further it is my contention that few military leaders or schools have made significant advances in intellectual areas. Although their administrative skills may be high, their lack of knowledge of the climate necessary for high-level research has meant that few have made lasting administrative contributions.

5 It has long been my contention that teaching in law schools is not only low-cost teaching but also is among the poorest examples in academia. The first difficulty may be in the excessive use of the case method, which requires much reading of numerous factual situations that are of little carryover value. The usual tradition for teaching is even worse: large classes and

impersonal professors who ask Student A for the facts of the case and then Student B for the legal issues, and then on to the next case. A number of educators have felt that perhaps one year of such detail is useful for practice in finding issues that are obscured by unbelievable underbrush, but few commend American lawyers for their interest in philosophy and the sociology of the law. Perhaps this broader background is supposed to come from undergraduate work, but the fact remains that our lawyers – so important in the American political scene – are pitifully educated when compared with their European counterparts.

6 *Editors' Note*: In Carl's original manuscript he left a blank space after "Plato's," so we don't know what specific reference Carl intended. He may have had a more specific reference in mind, for example, *The Republic*, the Academy at Athens, etc. Harvey inserted a generic reference "philosophy."

7 California seems to have an imperfect but reasonably effective system. Research and related activities are concentrated in the university system with emphasis on intellectual effort and originality. The state university (now a second-level system) puts more emphasis on undergraduate teaching and student work. The community (junior) colleges have been unusually successful. So far as I know, the trade level still is deficient but is improving. This structure does not try to incorporate an impossible mix of objectives within the same institution. Perhaps, best of all is that more recognition and prestige are accorded to the higher intellectual activities but in the Platonian tradition some prestige is reserved for all levels.

8 One of the advantages of a larger general-purpose university is the degree of specialization that can be offered. The Accounting Department at Florida State University and many other universities permits a great deal of specialization, for example, from conceptual theory to tax preparation and routine auditing by teachers who are themselves specialized enough to know their topics. Students have a choice and in many universities the classes are small enough to provide the advantages of both specialization and individual attention.

9 Unfortunately local citizenry far too often has taken a predatory attitude toward faculty and students that goes far beyond athletics. Occasionally, local landlords and restaurateurs object to university-owned dormitories and eating facilities. Apparently they forget the increased property values and additional business from the present of such institutions. That political figures would take such complaints seriously is beyond understanding.

10 A word may be in order about recent so-called "brain brawls." This movement is an interesting development and in the right direction. Unfortunately, most such contests are little more than exercises in trivial recall. At the same time, sincere attempts to test ability to relate and associate – the bases for intellectual activity – are widely denigrated.

11 These particular cases are perhaps extreme. Medical instruction has been inefficient in the tradition of hospitals and prima donna professors. On the other extreme, law instruction, although cheap, must be among the worst in all universities. Classes traditionally are large, equipment except for burdensome textbooks and large libraries is minimal. Yet law schools do teach less-facts-more-thinking without individual attention.

12 This is not to deny that some high-level, primarily independent schools are devoted largely to teaching, for example, Amherst, Williams, Carleton,

Oberlin, New College, Reed, Antioch, Haverford, Swarthmore, Davidson, and others. These schools are in a special position for they have very bright students who are highly homogeneous in ability. The teacher in these cases is not the traditional drill sergeant but is more likely to be highly articulate, widely read, and attuned to the causes and attitudes of idealistic youth. It is probably safe to say that more pure or near pure research is done at either Harvard or Berkeley than at all these colleges combined. Perhaps their teachers enjoy relating and were never interested in research. After all, research work is lonely work.

13 There is an interesting development at the other end – the highly qualified end – of the spectrum. It is probably true that the really top applicants have offers of admittance and scholarships from several universities. Thus even MIT may get only 50 percent of those it accepts and many other excellent universities (e.g. California) may get only a third. It is ego destroying for an institution to get only 10 percent. The effect is failure to make offers to the better qualified prospects – a deadly situation.

14 This task is not an easy one, for late bloomers are an important fact in education. As a rule, I have examined transcripts to observe whether candidates have tended to avoid the more analytical and more difficult courses when undergraduate options have been offered. If he has taken such courses, his grades relative to grades in more descriptive courses can sometimes indicate a lack of analytical ability. Occasionally, the trend of his undergraduate grades may be a much better predictor. If undergraduate work has been interrupted, a comparison of grades before and after sometimes reveals a change in attitude. Yet some students fail to get the idea during four years of study. Even here there is some chance that playboy attitudes have changed, but the evaluator's task is difficult indeed.

15 There are important exceptions to these generalizations. In the 1960s the economists in the University of Chicago School of Business were clearly better than most pure economics departments at most American universities, and at Carnegie-Mellon many organization theorists have made contributions to political science, psychology, and sociology.

16 *Editors' Note*: SIRS refers to the Student Instructor Rating System, a questionnaire developed at the University of Michigan. This evaluation form was the one utilized by The Florida State University for gathering student evaluations of their instructors.

17 We are not concerned here with the more widely understood problem of student evaluation – the various grading schemes. The intertwined, interdependent morass of three-way evaluation reminds some of the old vaudeville routine involving the permutations of "rustlers rustling rasslers."

18 It is true that a few authoritarian institutions discouraged criticism of their administrators and in other (usually older and better universities) the faculties often resented interference from any quarter, and the questionable tenure system was developed to head off administrative interference. Students traditionally have had the worst forum, yet the Michigan Graduate School of Business Administration had formal faculty evaluation sheets in the middle thirties, and once at a Christmas party presented the dean (a frustrated professor) with a small tree bearing a note: "a bush to beat around." Whether these particular evaluations were helpful to anyone may be seriously questioned, but I can vouch for the careful

thought that the student body devoted to them and to their therapeutic value for releasing resentment and frustration.

19 Yet in the American example further safeguards for orderly continuity are incorporated in the structure as a recognition that democracy may be inherently unstable. Congress may indeed swing more than is desired every two years, but executives are up every four years, senators for six years, and supreme court justices have lifetime appointments that usually cover several senatorial spans.

20 We are not concerned here with the question as to whether professional administrators even with all available helps are generally able to judge the quality of intellectual ability accurately enough to be entrusted with this important decision. In general, we feel that the skills of quick, decisive decisions and the like that make a good administrator are precisely the opposite of those of a scholar. The stubborn adherence to standards needed for scholarship are not concerned with the function of administrators to present and support the views of nonintellectual forces in a university's day-to-day operations, for example, the trustees, the tax payers, and the secretarial and janitorial help. Clearly administrators have important duties in all these directions.

21 In the past rural folks were more insistent on such free entertainment. Now with television and other alternatives it may be that the necessity for preachers and politicians to be entertaining may have decreased. Yet the opposite may be true, for students may be so accustomed to being passive and being entertained that they cannot function adequately in the classroom without it. Incidentally many politicians are now charging fees for their "addresses." Perhaps this change is due to the entrenched positions of so many incumbents so that pleasing the electorate is now less important.

22 I am reminded of an early experience in which a demure young student – apparently without guile – suggested that to be successful we should try to sell ourselves.

23 At the beginning of Second World War, students at Johns Hopkins protested the removal of a young instructor who they considered to be very entertaining. It turned out that he was effective at rolling his eyes in the manner of Eddie Kantor and performed interesting tricks such as stuffing New Year's honkers up his nose and blowing vigorously to emphasize occasional points. His class attendance was up, and some students were enthralled. There is no evidence that the evaluating committee considered these activities, but it did decide that his ability to expand the frontiers of learning was considerably less than his ability to transmit knowledge.

24 I do not wish to deny the need for substantive materials and stress on useful applications at any level, and I am not objecting to lower-level courses that contain much such material. A former calculus teacher was fond of summarizing his semester course by writing what the student should learn and later what he should have learned on the blackboards of one room. How many teachers in advanced fields may have felt that they could teach the entire course the first day and wonder how they were going to be able to fill out future lectures?

25 As a student I belonged to the latter group and was not at all concerned with whether or not I liked or disliked a particular professor so long as he had something that I wanted to know or understand. As a professor,

before the Berkeley affair of the sixties, I usually appealed to the offbeat, groping student who often was alienated or impatient with the chamber-of-commerce professor. Unfortunately, the Berkeley experience convinced me that a substantial number of students – perhaps not even a majority – were actually anti-intellectual and were therefore direct enemies of the ideas I tried to espouse.

26 I always have thought that the approach used at Michigan and Wharton was ideal for genuine university students. One good demonstration problem of each major kind was followed by a homework problem of the same general type. For some students too much drill (studying with the head of a pencil) can be deadly.

27 Emile Durkheim was deeply concerned, well over a half-century ago, with this question in terms of the division of labor and function in society. "How are we to ensure that a society divided among innumerable specialists will retain the necessary intellectual and moral coherence?" Raymond Aron, *Main Currents in Sociological Thought* (New York: Basic Books Inc., 1967). Durkheim's position is found in *De la division du travail social – The Division of Labor in Society* (English version originally published, New York: Macmillan, 1933). This problem area has dramatically resurfaced recently as (*Editors' Note*: Carl never completed this thought in the original manuscript).

28 *Editors' Note*: See "Dissident Literature and the Absurd," Part II of Essay 3 in *Carl Thomas Devine: Essays in Accounting Theory – A Capstone*, ed. H. S. Hendrickson (New York: Garland Publishing, Inc., 1999) pp. 55–73.

8 Rational models and subjective probability assessments[1]

Rational models with their accompanying assumption of optimality and maximization have all but taken over the field of economics and are by far the most important framework for decisions in management science and accounting. This essay takes a critical look at the maximizing of individual objectives as an organization paradigm and as a surrogate and even as justification for human ethics. I have always argued that some amount of rationality must be posited in order to avoid a world of chaos and to bring about some semblance of order to human actions, and that effort should be made to specify the conditions necessary for the converging of individual and social goals. Less attention has been directed to this vital congruence in terms of ethical discourse.

The following analyses of the rationality assumption proceeds along four fronts. First, at the lowest level the premise itself is non-operational in that there is no independent way to test the assumption and to assess its influence (perhaps the recent statistical tests for system sensitivity to change in assumptions can be of limited help). Second, there is no warrant for assuming that pursuing individual objectives by a short-run process that optimizes each decision will lead to optimizing over the long run. Third, severe restrictions are necessary before concluding that pursuit of individual welfare at every decision point (even if successful) will lead to a satisfactory level of welfare for all aggregations of individuals. Fourth, from an ethical perspective there is no reason to believe that concentrating on maximizing economic scarcity values is more desirable than alternative organizing schemes that include other noneconomic freely shared values. Clearly, the use of models to support ethical positions is highly suspect.

It is not the objective in this essay to discuss Karl Popper's distinction between comprehensive and critical rationality (*The Open Society and*

Its Enemies (Princeton: Princeton University Press, various editions, 1945)). This opposition of *total* planning systems and *piecemeal* systems has never been appealing even though it has received renewed interest in C. West Churchman's *The Systems Approach and Its Enemies* (New York: Basic Books, 1979) and in Charles Christenson's excellent analytical review.

In my opinion, Churchman's commitment to *total* systems that insists that everything is connected has been a serious mistake. Fear of committing his "environmental fallacy" has proved to be a barrier to fruitful inquiry and an unnecessary bogeyman for your scholars. It is clearly necessary that all serious inquiry omit unimportant variables, admit constraining parameters, and attempt to randomize other features. In short, successful inquiry requires the severance of a portion of the environment for manageable study and the careful suturing of the open wounds. According to Christenson, Churchman acknowledges, in effect the self-contradictory nature of this worldview, saying that "Eventually the disciple must commit the environmental fallacy, since he believes that what is outside the position and the theme does not exist or is meaningless, ridiculous, inappropriate; his worldview – for him – has no environment."[2] Unfortunately some of Churchman's own disciples (e.g. Mattessich) have insisted that interconnectivity within and sharp separation of the system from the environment are *the* significant defining properties of the systems approach. It should be clear that the appropriate size of a system of inquiry is a variable that must be adjusted to the importance of the study, and the scope of available cognitive abilities at hand. The inclusion of more and more variables does not invariably lead to more useful research.

The charge that the rationality assumption is nonoperational is an old criticism and as with other such nostrums is only partially true. The difficulties are simple enough. The inquirer can never be sure whether an actor is acting rationally or irrationally, that is, so that the expected outcomes will maximize or even optimize his well-being. It may be that the outcomes were unknown or unexpected so that he may have been trying to maximize his welfare but fell short due to ignorance or some chance factors in the relationship among antecedent actions and actual consequences. Perhaps, his decisions were rational enough but the implementing actions were unintentional or faulty. The objectives may have been ordered rationally but due to ignorance or to random and overlapping factors were not consistent and do not need the restrictions necessary for determining mathematical optimality.

Some empirical evidence can be brought to bear in these situations. Researchers can *inquire* about individual objectives and their perceived tradeoff values. Answers can be supplemented by inferences of various sorts from related actions and decisions. In a similar fashion, actors can be asked about the consequences expected from their decisions in order to isolate possible unexpected outcomes. Finally, the individual or the researcher may be able to recognize faulty operations that were not concealed with decision plans.

Clearly, these problems do not belong to rational maximizing models alone. All alternatives are subject to similar ambiguities and nonoperational features. From an ethical perspective, there is nothing fundamentally wrong about the assumption that all individuals are rational and are attempting to maximize their utilities. Clearly, the assumption is not a fact until it has been established as a valid representation of each particular motivation and behavior. More important for an ethicist is whether such a model represents a desirable state of the human condition.

Even with the most modern techniques of inquiry some questions and doubts always remain. Even the best well-ordered set of objectives (ends in view) are themselves means to further ends. Thus, the process must be repeated and the rational being must continue the regress until he has some sort of specifiable far off, ultimate set of objectives, for example, happiness, the good life. In the process he must relate each prior set of objectives – now acting as means – to his *final* set and in so doing order the tradeoff value of each in view of both expected and unexpected consequences. At all stages ignorance and ineptness are strong factors.

In an ethical context the individual's system of values is taken as supreme. It is not necessary to impose an independent ethical system as a basis for judgment. The positivistic framework compares outcomes with objectives to determine whether or not individuals are rational in pursuing their perceived objectives. At the lowest level positivists attempt only to observe outcomes. A major jump is required to associate an observed set of outcomes with possible causes and to place events in an antecedent–consequence format. Still a greater leap is required to demonstrate that the antecedents were manipulated to produce consequences that further objectives. The final leap – impossible by positivist standards – is to demonstrate that the actor *ought* to manipulate the antecedents in the way they were, in fact, manipulated – and that others ought to act similarly.

Certainly, the complete separation of facts and judgments is impossible, for facts too are judgments and are dependent on perspective. Judgments, as Dewey explained, may all be value judgments, but they are not identical and may require separation according to the needs of the situation. Certainly, there is no important general implication that they are identical except on their methodological requirements. Judgments of all kinds are made by different individuals, acting in different capacities, at different hierarchical levels, and to accomplish objectives that may be entirely different. Thus, it is necessary to examine them, classify them, and order them for their relevance and importance for any inquiry at hand.

Digression: subjective probabilities

Consider now some aspects of "subjective" probability and the feeling that maximizing expected values will somehow lead to preferred outcomes. Specifically consider whether a rational person seeking optimum satisfaction should try to maximize expected values as reflected by the product of conditional values (i.e. the numerical value if the outcome is favorable) and the subjective expectation (probability) of a favorable outcome. Both of these beliefs are based on probability estimates made according to definite rules and constrained by certain obvious assumptions about the appropriate mathematical manipulations. The serious question is not whether such beliefs should be considered – of course they should – the question here is whether the usual mathematical expectation is a superior means for reaching rational maximization.

For many decades, it has been my contention that all probability theory is subjective and differs only in degree from modern definitions of subjective probability. Certainly, the evidence for belief may differ widely with the situation. Sometimes, belief is supported by selecting a geometrical shape, and then, with the assumption that all side conditions for each situation are equal, asserting a definite limiting probability number. For example, a perfect cube may be expected to converge in the long haul to one in six. Physicists may with stipulated conditions support by deduction the expected number, but in practice the same numbers may be supported by simple observation with allowances for dissimilar side conditions. Since no cube is perfect the empirical procedure also helps prediction when the die is imperfect or the side conditions are not similar. What about odd shape objects, for example, six-sided objects with irregular, concave, or convex surfaces? Here the geometricians are of less help and the traditional procedure is to employ observation with the usual assumptions of stable convergence tendencies. Thus, both cases are or can be treated empirically and both require subjective assessment. Clearly there is no easy answer here.

It may be useful as a preliminary step to remind the reader that the writer is a hopeless subjectivist who believes that the individual has an important part in all observation, understandings, realities, and decisions. Objectivity is limited to the use of analogies to serve as models or mechanical devices to settle decisions about limited parts of the inquiry.

Consider, for example, the objective nature of the usual university objective examination. The instructor decides subjectively what materials are to be covered in the scope of the test. He then (again subjectively) decides which questions are appropriate for covering the course material. He further decides the weights to be assigned for each question. In "objective" test the weights are usually equal. He decides which answers will be acceptable and which not. He decides how many tests are sufficient and which areas can be safely omitted. Finally he decides acceptable gradations that can be used for pass–fail; A, B, C, D and F, and the like. After the subjective decisions have been made the test is then said to be an objective examination and turned over to subordinates or machine for grading.

Consider now the extension of probability theory to the current field of subjective probability. In practice, experience with assessing similarities and side conditions can be expected but often belief is supported by geometrical and physical analog. These helps are not available in subjective probability. The common feature here is that decisions are to be made with a methodology that is common to all. The dependence on methodology here is stark indeed. The outcomes are not simple observations such as heads–tails or symbols printed on cards. In subjective probability the conditional values also may be variable, and the probabilities may differ for each trial. Furthermore, the constraints of (supposedly) identical conditions means that historical analogues are often diverse.

In spite of these difficulties some sort of convergence is assumed in order to apply the stipulated conditions for probability theory. Convergence to what? What is it that converges? (Converges on the best profit position?) What is it that the decisions have in common? What do the outcomes have in common? How can we assume that each try (decision) is more or less identical or at least similar? Do the people who make the decisions need to be identical? In what ways? Is the requirement for a common method the most important justifying variable? Can we reach a broad general concept of maximization of welfare without including instructions for selecting the best personnel for estimating? It may not matter who throws the dice so long as common procedures are used to approximate randomness. The probabilities in subjective decision making in businesses certainly do depend on the judgment of the decision-makers.

Perhaps the solutions attained by modern decision theory are the *best* only for a particular decision-maker and should not be generalized to cover different situations. Perhaps decision-maker A would be better off by consulting an astrologer, a consistent astrologer! The questions go on and on.

Obviously, there is a heavy burden on the concept of methodology and on the particular methods employed. Optimization and maximization require estimating and comparing sacrifices and benefits, but these measurements and comparisons are difficult and depend on the perspective taken. Benefits often run to certain individuals while sacrifices are imposed on others so that some degree of interpersonal interaction is necessary for effective comparison. Measurement too offers severe problems. All accountants are aware that the measurement of cost depends on the baseline employed – short-run marginal costs measured from current conditions certainly differ from long-run average costs that take a longer view and start with entirely different conditions. Thus, maximization for whom as well as optimizing over what period are both relevant.

The general conclusion at this point is that the maximizing model is far from being a total (general) model. It may or may not be helpful to know that the solution is optimum even though the wrong personnel are involved. A more general model would provide for the selection of the best people available to make the decisions. So far no explicit expansion has been forthcoming but in the practical world of business, a sort of social Darwinism may be at work to get rid of those who estimate poorly.

Finally, consider the timing as well as the time-span of the optimizing model. How does one know that a different time horizon or a different order of decisions would not lead to greater optimization? It is not at all clear that following best beliefs at each interval will be consistent with or better than beliefs made for longer intervals. Rationality certainly does not imply clairvoyance but the model does presume that following best judgments at each decision part will yield the best long-run results. Presumably, all future contingencies with appropriate discount factors are somehow incorporated in all sequential decisions. Furthermore, some sort of invisible hand guides the whole operation. What about information that might become available if the decisions were delayed? Statisticians have devised ways to differentiate some of these cases but belief in the conclusions requires considerable methodological faith.[3]

So far we have not discussed the ethical aspects of optimization, maximization, and rationalization. With an assumption of unequal ability of individuals rational beings become more efficient at accomplishing their goals (whatever they are) so that they may end up with an inordinate share of the wealth. In this respect the unfortunate unrationals may not only end up with less well-being but they may also suffer from recognizing and resenting their rational inferiority. On the other hand, perhaps the more fortunate will share their good fortune or, better yet, the unfortunates become not so unfortunate and can be trained to utilize the more efficient models. This criticism applies to all social arrangements for all systems have some implicit (in addition as any explicit) allocations of the things that make up the good life. Capitalistic economics reward groups with certain skills and abilities through consumer and producer surpluses, one-price trading, marginal allocation, and the like. Socialist economics may make those with less talent feel exhilarated but leave those with greater abilities terribly disturbed.

It is true that there are positivistic defenders of maximization and optima. It is not necessary that the objective function (goals) be selected in any particular fashion to benefit any particular group so long as the objectives can be specified in a manner that fits the model. Even if all the population were competent to use these models they should still have different objective functions so that diverse goals remain necessary. If abilities are distributed optimally then the accomplishments should be distributed in a satisfactory manner, but this question to positivists is a separate question – a question of social welfare and ethics.

Digression: populations and universes

Some decades ago, I became concerned with the nature and extent of universes that are represented by a particular sampling method. This concern came into focus with a look at non-parametric methods but it is clearly present in other sampling arrangements as well.

So long as a population is known in advance there is little problem beyond finding how well various types of sampling techniques and simplifications represent the population to be described. By taking complete enumeration of the important attributes certain aspects of the universe can be taken as true according to a widely used definition of truth. Usually the sampling operations along with the results must be subjected to observation and comparison so that philosophically the grounding is a dualistic world that furnishes the required attributes and a set of observers who can sense the presence, absence of relative density of such characteristics.

Now when the population is known or specified, the boundaries are in less but not without dispute. Yet, members of the universe are not and cannot be identical in all respects for it is a commonplace that every entity differs from others in many aspects. The problem then becomes one of specifying the attributes of interest and setting the limits of the universe in terms that can be observed classified and made subject to certain elementary rules of arithmetic. In short the stipulated universe is bounded by some recognizable limits and in later research observed for the presence or absence of these stipulated characteristics. Again philosophically the universe is (or can be) known with respect to inclusion and with regard to attributes that human senses can distinguish. The classes seem to be unique and exhaustive when subject to observation.

After accepting these restrictions the inquirer can then devote himself to the simpler task of deciding how well and in what ways these samples describe the simplified universe. Of course, the specified population, say apples in a particular basket sampled in a specified fashion for a certain attribute at a particular time can act only as an analogy for other baskets under different conditions. Generalization depends largely on the related decision as to the homogeneity of the situations and the whole process thus depends on the assumptions of the nearness of analogies. This analogy certainly becomes blurred if the generalization extends to all apples for an entire season for the whole world.

Philosophically, the problem gets interesting when the universe is defined entirely by the sampling methods applied to a limited area. Presumably the universe extends to all cases in which similar sampling methods could be applied. In turn this decision depends on judgments about the homogeneity of the members that might be covered. The boundaries of the universe may be set by stipulation, and the stipulation to be useful requires the judgment as to the effective limits of homogeneity. Perhaps what is needed is some measure or systematic estimate of the density of similarity as the universe is extended further and further from the samples that are actually sampled. Thus one should always be concerned about possible diversity as one moves away from the actual population that makes up the sample.

Observe that in descriptive statistics the inquirer stipulates the universe to be tested, the definitions to be used, the characteristics to be observed, and the process for combining the observations. Thus descriptive statistics describe only a limited number of attributes (presumably attributes of real interest and concern) in a specific language that specifies and more or less certifies the nature of the process and the physical actions necessary for the process to work. Thus the sampling simplification of a population is assumed to be an adequate simplification for immediate needs and objectives.

Shorthand summaries of some common attributes from different batches of data are certainly useful but curious inquirers may wish to go further. Unless the populations are specified and identifiable on some physical basis such as successive production batches, researchers may wish to know something about the boundaries of the universes that have been sampled. The case may become more interesting when probabilities are involved where it is also necessary to know something about the boundaries of the universes to which the probability estimates may be rightfully applied. Observe that this problem is separate from the usual questions of independence among members and the selection rules needed to perform the judgments. These rules include instructions for identifying members, agreeing on the presence or absence of the attributes of interest, and the like.

In the interesting area of estimating the limits of the populations and therefore the extent to which the inferences may be extended the discussions have been less precise and more open-ended. The populations by default are defined implicitly by the specification of the sampling *process* employed. Certainly if one wishes to know something about the useful extent of his probability estimates he must know something about the range over which his sampling applies. Unless he wishes to assume a universe of uniform density with sharp borders he must be prepared to include cases in which the borders, like ocean waves, continue with diminishing or perhaps changing intensity until they are so vague that their characteristics can no longer be measured, discerned, or even estimated. Actually, the density is assumed to be represented by the parameters that are specified in the sampling process and continue until the researcher decides – on some other not so clear basis – that the information and inferences no longer apply. How is this decision made with open-ended populations?

Consider now the comparison of two open-ended populations that have been sampled by the identical or near identical sampling process. How does he even decide whether he even has two populations? Certainly, there must be some reason and basis for believing that the populations are separate, and since the sampling rules must be similar this decision must be made on other criteria. Some differences must be identified and brought into focus so that the distinction can be made empirically. Clearly, it should have some significance for the research effort.

With unknown populations the universes are closed either by stipulation or implicitly by the rules adopted from the sampling process. The sample thus speaks for any population that meets the conditions set forth in the sampling design. Suppose for an illustration that a sample of the crow population in a certain meadow at specified hours with supplementary restrictions and conditions such as what constitutes a crow (eggs?), the boundaries of the field, and the state of the weather. The inquirer will ordinarily want to draw broader inferences. How do the results apply, for example, to different days with different weather conditions? To adjoining fields? To remote fields with different growth and pasture? To fields on the West coast? In North America? To the World? To canaries and eagles? To non-mating seasons? These are the extensions that are sometimes desired, although in many cases the area of inquiry is concerned only with the particular conditions at hand. In most important cases, however, the knowledge sought requires judgment and inference to some larger determinate by undetermined population.

In short, the extension of conclusions must require some extraneous observations and conclusions about the similarity of populations in some important aspects. Otherwise, any extension borders on the vacuous by asserting that to the extent conditions in the populations are similar, conclusions are warranted.

Subjective probability

The interesting questions surrounding subjective probability arises about the possible warrant for assuming that all sorts of decisions made at different times at different places with different mental attitudes will lead to optimizing conditions because the goal of maximum profit along with the method of procedure remain unchanged. Thus, the conditions may be entirely different so *long* as possible outcomes share in common some perceived ability to satisfy the decision-maker's needs. Actually these needs may change radically from decision to decision, and the decision-maker's outlook – his relative optimism and pessimism – cannot be expected to remain constant. Even the decision-maker or the committee may not remain identical over any appreciable period. Presumably there is a sequential order in the decisions for each must take into consideration any expected changes in the value of all preceding resources. These possibilities need to be evaluated with even-handed assessments given other expected advantages.

Thus the most interesting question surrounding subjective probability is the possible warrant for assuming that all sorts of decisions at different times with different conditions are equivalent simply because the method of combining judgments remains unchanged. The individual situations may be entirely different so long as the possible outcomes have in common the ability to satisfy the decision-maker's objectives. Actually these objectives may themselves change from decision to decision, and certainly the maker's outlook – his pessimism and optimism and his assessment abilities – cannot be expected to remain constant. Furthermore, there is some kind of sequential order in the decisions for each must take into consideration any changes in the value of existing resources – the heritage problem.

A further feature is worth noting, that is, the imposition of the maximizing assumption and the method used to arrive at expectations may themselves influence the estimates as well as the search for possible alternatives. The usual decision theory text usually examines the maximization tendency of the model even with incomplete information but it does not point out that the maximization model itself is problematic and may influence search activity and therefore the information that becomes available. Clearly, a satisfying model that attempts to constrain certain areas while maximizing others may lead to far different informational inputs so that efforts to process information and to refine probability estimates may be misdirected.

The problem becomes more complicated when there are ambiguities in the objective functions to be maximized. Normally, there is not just one clear-cut objective to be maximized and the various goals, for example, profit, cash flow, growth, must be amalgamated in some fashion. The mechanics of programming constraints and modern algebra may be of limited use but sooner or later the decision-maker must make the necessary tradeoffs to combine them. General simplifying constraints to be satisfied may help but they too must be integrated and decisions made about their relative importance. Finally, the strength of these competing and cooperating vectors may change so that each decision must consider different initial conditions and values. Modern algebraic methods certainly may help with the arrangement of the judgments and offer help with the simplifications but so far as I know there has been no general method of allowing for dynamic changes in the values from decision to decision.

What then is the warrant for assuming that maximization of some measure of subjective well-off-ness at each opportunity by the use of any well-defined method will lead to an optimal position or even to a preferred condition? Normally there are reasons for selecting any end in view and the methods for obtaining it. These reasons may or may not be convincing to others or even to the decision-maker himself at other times. Sometimes the bases for belief in finding successful outcomes by procedural means are so vague that some sweeping general or semantic grounding is invented. The creation of the invisible hand may have been the product of economists who wish to convince the public (and perhaps themselves) that the pursuit of self-interest by individuals redounds to the benefit of the social group. Psychologists fall back on urges, yens, dispositions, and the like to support some of their theories. Economists use tendencies and the usual attributes associated with some assumed economic man. Physicists rely on symmetries and associations beyond ordinary imagination. Theoretically, mathematicians often simply stipulate the necessary influences and limit their models by simple if–then conditions.[4]

No two situations are alike so that in all rational decisions belief must be supported by all sorts of analogies with other more widely accepted structures and with some accepted similarities. An invisible hand as an operational concept is not very useful but as a semantic shorthand for some mysterious set of forces it may have strong persuasive powers. Attempts to explain the forces behind the invisible hands have not been of notable success but they usually allude indirectly to natural forces, God's intervention and plan, psychological conditioning, or any other set of possible explanations for what are essentially unexplainable beliefs.

The support for subjective probability comes primarily from analogy with more "objective" probability beliefs. Yet even with cards and dice, the conditions are never identical and there may be serious questions about the similarity of the physical bases for belief, for example, differences in the cards and shuffles employed, and the possible physical defects in the surfaces, the density, and actual tossing of the dice. Belief in the probability numbers results from belief in the control system that leads to homogeneity of instances and the further belief that future conditions will be controlled in a similar manner.

Additional support may come from idealized conceptions of the shape of the dice, the productive quality control of the manufacture of the cards, etc. Yet these idealized supports are of the stipulated if–then variety and actual belief is usually supported by experience with similar situations. Odd-shaped dice and unknown wild cards call for revisions of belief and these revisions come from analogies and experience. Clearly, objective probability is an idealized chimera or a convenient label for a measure of consensus and as such it suffers from the same severe criticism that the term endures in all other usages.

What about physical analogies and experimental support for subjective probabilities in modern decision making?[5]

Notes

1 *Editors' Note*: Carl was not happy with this essay. His marginal notations on the original manuscript indicated he was thinking of scrapping it.
2 Charles Christenson, Book review of C. West Churchman, "The Systems Approach and Its Enemies," *Journal of Enterprise Management*, Vol. 3, No. 1, 1981, p. 199.
3 Traditionally the techniques of the calculus of variations have been applied to maximization and optimization problems. Sidney Morgenbesser points out the advantages of dynamic programming and control theory in some cases. See his "The Realist-Instrumentalist Controversy," *Philosophy, Science, and Method, Essays in Honor of Ernest Nagel* (New York: St Martin's Press, 1969), pp. 200–18. He cites Martin J. Bechmann, *Dynamic Programming for Economic Decisions* (Berlin: Springer-Verlag, 1968) for serious discussion.
4 It is possible that most idealists have underestimated the usefulness of greed and self-interest in our functioning social world. As one recent television commentator [*Editors' Note*: we were not able to determine to whom Carl was referring] puts it: Many obscure innovators and businessmen may have benefited mankind enough to be ranked with the very greatest moral leaders who rail at the profit system and believe only in agape and the benefits of grace and beneficence.
5 *Editors' Note*: The essay ends here. Carl was not able to finish it. Harvey Hendrickson decided the order of appearance of these eight essays. His thinking was that, though perhaps anticlimactic to end Carl's collection of essays with an unfinished one, it is an appropriate tribute to one whose search for understanding was never complete. Great teacher that he was, how better to conclude this seventh volume of Carl's essays than with a rhetorical question?

Index